*State House, Annapolis*

*Hammond-Harwood House, Annapolis*

# MY MARYLAND

## A. AUBREY BODINE

*Fellow of the Photographic Society of America*

Published by Bodine and Associates, Inc., Baltimore ★ Distributed by Hastings House Publishers, Inc., New York

*Washington Monument and Mount Vernon Place Methodist Church, Baltimore.*

Copyright 1952 by Bodine and Associates, Inc.
Made in U.S.A.

# FOREWORD

*This is a book about love.*

The word itself does not appear on any other page. But the statement is still true.

The world is so arranged that men must work. The man who finds abiding satisfaction in his work is fortunate indeed. But the man who falls in love with his work and never falls out again is a rarer creature. He is indeed blessed. And the world shares the blessing. For such a man produces, for the use and the delight of others, work that transcends the excellences of mere workmanship, however fine.

The creator of this book is one of these most fortunate of men.

Combine the qualities of authentic genius with lifelong love of a chosen work. Add to that a sense of beauty and of drama and excitement. Add to that the rarest of all forms of the imagination—sensitivity. The sum of these is Aubrey Bodine.

And this book is the sum of Bodine. It is the summed-up richness of the work of twenty-five years.

If you count the pictures in it, you will come to the conclusion that there are one hundred and seventy-four. The number will be correct; but it will also be quite wrong. No set of numerals can express the contents of this book. For what you hold in your hands is the essence of twenty-five thousand photographs—the best of Bodine produced in a quarter of a century.

If you have a fondness for facts and statistics, there is ample store of them. A. Aubrey Bodine is the photographic director of the Baltimore Sun's unique Sunday Magazine. All of the pictures in "My Maryland" were made for The Sunpapers. They include forty-five photographs of Baltimore in its amazing range of moods, and one hundred and twenty-nine scenes drawn from all the Free State's twenty-three counties.

The man who made them has won international recognition as a distinguished artist. He has won the first prize in competitions that drew more than fifty thousand entries. He has won awards in England and India, Belgium and Brazil, Canada and Sweden, Spain and Cuba. Fifteen of his photographs are on permanent exhibit at the Smithsonian.

But the facts and the statistics really tell you nothing. The truth that makes this book a thing of beauty is that it is the story of a man's love—his lifelong love of chosen work. The truth that makes this book great is that the pictures it contains were not made by the sensitivity of lens and chemicals and shutter. They were taken by the heart of a man.

*Neil H. Swanson*

DAYBREAK ON THE ATLANTIC SHORE

# MY MARYLAND

IF YOU were to look at a map of the United States you would find that, of all the states, Maryland has the oddest shape. Some states are long and thin, others almost perfectly square and some entirely irregular, but Maryland is almost cut in two, and not just once, but twice. The majestic Chesapeake Bay, with its thousands of estuaries and its 3600 miles of coastline, divides the state into the "Eastern Shore" and the "Western Shore." Farther west, in Washington County, the state is pinched into a wasp waist only four miles wide, and from a proper vantage point Pennsylvania, West Virginia, and Maryland can all be seen at one time, as in the picture on page 113.

Maryland is a fascinating place, both from a scenic and from a photographic point of view. It is not without reason called "America in Miniature."

From the bay the land sweeps ever higher into beautiful, rolling farmland, and through the western counties the Appalachian Mountains heave it into a crazy quilt pattern. A Free State resident is fortunate, for these contrasting natural wonders are within a few hours' drive of each other.

Roaming and probing around the state for the last quarter of a century for the Sunpapers, I have amassed a wealth of material—and there is just as much or more still to be photographed and written about. Many persons have asked me, "When are you going to do a pictorial history of Maryland?" I hope this book will provide the answer.

I have selected the pictures with the end in view of attempting to tell as complete a story as possible of Maryland's three centuries of growth and independence, her people, and their activities. Obviously there are omissions; there must be, unless one has thousands of pages at his disposal. I have tried to select those things which spoke to me most strongly of Maryland, oftentimes passing up something obvious for something more obscure but more meaningful. It has been a tremendous task to select 174 pictures from the twenty-five thousand I have made, especially when each one of them has in it something of importance.

I sincerely hope the reader will enjoy the selection made and forgive the omissions which space has made necessary.

There is only one "personal" picture in the book and that is the picture of St. Mark's Episcopal Church in Washington County, which appears on page 121. It was in this church that my father, Joel Goode Bodine, married my mother, Louise A. Wilson, in June, 1904. My great-grandfather, George Scott Kennedy, contributed toward building the parish in its early years. Even without this family connection, however, I would have included the picture, because the church is very quaint and pretty.

Another of my favorite church pictures, that on page 118, was made at Cumberland. For those of you who are photographically inclined, the view was made possible through the use of a lens of enormous focal length—twenty-eight inches—and infrared film to cut the haze.

A third church picture was made under unusual circumstances: that of the Catholic Cathedral on page 60. This was taken during one of the heaviest snowfalls ever recorded in Baltimore—the twenty-two inch one of Palm Sunday, 1942. Only from inside the closed Pratt Library, opposite, could I get the elevation I desired; and because Miss Kate Coplan, of the library staff, was her usual obliging self the library was opened to me. It was an opportunity seized in the nick of time, for under a bright sun the next day the snow vanished as swiftly as it had come.

In doing a book of this kind it is necessary to check every statement, and I was often struck by the lack of agreement among reference sources on the state. For instance, the spelling of "Sotterley," a picture of which appears on page 74, is not uniform. H. D. Richardson's "Sidelights of Maryland History," J. W. Thomas's "Chronicles of Colonial Maryland," the WPA's "Maryland Guide," and Hulbert Footner's "Maryland Main and the Eastern Shore" at one important place, all spell it "Sotterly," which I found by further research to be incorrect. I have tried hard to make this book free from error.

"Sotterley" is one of the finest restored homes in Maryland. Many old houses are still awaiting restoration by people with patience, good taste and a fairly substantial bank account. Of them all, the early home "Anderton" (page 16) I feel to be one of the most interesting. This "skull buster," with its tiny doors, is unique in the state.

"Doughoregan Manor," page 96, is a great three hundred foot mansion. Reference works seemed to disagree concerning the number of generations of Carrolls that have lived there. The way out of this confusion was simple: I inquired of Philip Carroll, the present squire. He is of the seventh generation. Incidentally, he is currently rehabilitating the soil through scientific methods.

Were I personally to have my choice of all the old Colonial homes, I believe I would select "Otwell," page 17. Although it does not have the majestic, formal appearance of many Colonial and Georgian homes, it does have a sense of informal, sincere, mellow welcome suggesting to me that here is a house to live in and enjoy.

One type of building that probably will not be seen much longer is the little wooden schoolhouse. There are a number of them in the state, but they are rapidly passing out of existence as the new consolidated schools are built. The little schoolhouse shown on page 21 was photographed on a trip through Caroline County with David Lampe, who has an exceptional knowledge of Maryland history and folklore.

Rather recent newcomers to Maryland, as time goes, are the Amish, who have settled in St. Marys County. One does not ask the Amish to pose for pictures— nor do the gentle people consent if asked; their religion forbids them to pose for any kind of image. The picture shown on page 73 was made at a distance of six feet, with the camera hanging carelessly alongside my hip, while the children were watching a birdhouse being erected. They did not know their picture had been taken. Note the absence of buttons on the clothing; only hooks and eyes are used by these fine people, who love freedom and the land.

Some of the big events of my life took place on Tilghman Island when, as a boy, I visited my uncle, Dr. Scott Kennedy Wilson; once he took me to St. Michaels and purchased for me my first pair of long pants. The picture I made at Tilghman (page 32) shows an oyster tonger at work among the ruins of a steamboat wharf. Many summers ago I would eagerly watch for the arrival of the steamer, which was first announced by a huge plume of black smoke visible miles away.

Boats were romantic to the boy I was then. Nowadays I can also appreciate such things as the beautiful pastel hue of some of the brick houses in the charming town of Frederick. The shade is a unique dilution of red that I do not recall having seen elsewhere, and I feel it is something that decorators would do well to look into. Many of the Frederick houses are gems; some are of log construction, since covered with clapboard, and others are of all types, many with quaint dormer windows.

I can still recall one of the last runs of the Baltimore-Washington steamboat. The steamer Dorchester left Baltimore Saturday afternoon and arrived in Washington on Monday morning. The fare was $12.12, which included meals, stateroom and a train ticket to get the traveler back to Baltimore. The rail journey took an hour. Many stops were made on the boat trip, taking on a calf, leaving off a coffin and picking up and discharging sundry cargoes. Some of the old bay steamers are shown on pages 42 and 43.

Another boat trip, one of the pleasantest assignments I have ever had, was one aboard the four-master Doris Hamlin to Newport News (see frontispiece). Because of calms and light winds, it took an entire week to make Newport News. Upon arrival there, I boarded an Old Bay Line boat and was back in Baltimore the next morning. That trip was made in 1939. The following year the Doris Hamlin, loaded with coal and carrying a crew of ten, set out for the Canary Islands. She disappeared at sea and not a trace of her or her crew has been found to this day.

The Valiant Lady (page 26) was photographed during a race on the Miles River. I shot the picture from another boat, and during the next race boarded the Valiant Lady to get some close-ups of the crew in action. I was supposed to be mere ballast, but I had to turn into a bailer. The boat had purposely been left on shore for some days to dry out, on the logical theory that she would be much lighter for racing. Little did anyone expect that the 85-year-old seams would open up enough to let water in!

The letting out of water resulted in a spectacular picture in another instance (page 103). This was at the great Conowingo dam, on the one occasion since its erection when all fifty-three gates had to be opened to let a mighty Susquehanna flood roll through. From the foot of the dam this was a very thrilling and awe inspiring sight, and the roar was thunderous.

At Lilypons (page 108) floods of a different sort are put to use. Fields have been flooded and tanks built for the raising of goldfish and water lilies. Lilypons is a beautiful place to visit during the summer, when hundreds of thousands of water lilies are in bloom. The enterprise is nestled between Sugar Loaf Mountain and the Monocacy River. The whole countryside throughout this section is like toyland, with beautiful farmhouses and barns set out in orderly fashion, many enclosed by stone walls.

Maryland's first city, St. Marys, is almost a ghost town today. One of my maternal ancestors, Gerret Van Sweringen, seven generations back, settled there after fleeing from New Amstrel, now New Castle, Delaware. He became an alderman, then high sheriff and proprietor of the first tavern in the colony. He was required by a town ordinance to maintain twelve feather beds and provide stables for twenty horses. A replica of the first capitol building at St. Marys is shown on page 78.

The last picture in the book, titled "Insomnia," was made at Jericho Farm, near Boonsboro, my mother's family home, where many pleasant times were enjoyed over the years before it passed from Wilson hands. All of the lights in the house were darkened except one; the camera was opened after the moon rose over South Mountain and the picture made.

*A. Aubrey Bodine, F.P.S.A.*

*Baltimore, Maryland, November, 1952*

THE EARLY BIRD GETS THE FISH . . . Surf casters on Assateague Island below Ocean City get up with the sun to try their luck. This sport comes in when the first chill of fall strikes the Atlantic; not only high boots, but sweaters and windbreakers are common fishing garb. The prize sought is the gamy channel bass, which may run well over forty pounds in weight. The scales of this fish, incidentally, are so big and hard, and so strongly attached that Assateaguers use a garden hoe to remove them.

EAST-WEST . . . On the bleak, sandy plains of Assateague Island, south of Ocean City, cattle roam at will, little disturbed by man—until round-up time. Hundreds of wild ponies also roam this long, narrow strip of ocean-swept land. Every July many of the ponies are driven across a small inlet and auctioned off on the island of Chincoteague. These are known as Chincoteague ponies. The origin of the ponies is unknown; a legend says a Spanish shipwreck cast a few ashore years ago.

STRONGARM FERRY . . . The cable ferry pictured here plies back and forth over the Wicomico River at the village of Upper Ferry. It is one of three small arm-powered craft still in use on this Eastern Shore waterway. When large boats approach, moving up- or down-river, the cables are dropped to the bottom of the stream, and the boats pass over them. At nearby Whitehaven a fourth ferry originally operated by hand has been modernized by the addition of outboard motors.

BLACK WATER . . . The early Indians named the Pocomoke River and named it well, for a translation of the word means "Black Water." Flowing as it does through cypress groves and the great Pocomoke Swamp, the water picks up a very dark brown color from the bog. It is Maryland's deepest fresh water river and for its width, may well be the deepest in the United States. It seems also to be a demarcation line between northern and southern forms of both bird and plant life and its environs teem with wildlife.

Pocomoke River, Worcester County

IRON THEN . . . Nassawango Furnace, Worcester County, was erected in 1832 to smelt the bog ore of Nassawango Creek. In a short time more than one hundred houses, a hotel and stores were built around it. When better, cheaper ores were mined elsewhere the boom town collapsed, then gradually disappeared. All that remains is the furnace, which was abandoned in 1847.

STEEL NOW . . . In contrast to bygone days this Bessemer converter roars in fury in the huge, sprawling plant of the Bethlehem Steel Company at Sparrows Point. The men, dwarfed by the tremendous structures, work ore that comes from as far away as Venezuela.

TOMATOLAND . . . Picked, packed, canned and cooked all in one day. That is what happens to most of Maryland's whole tomato crop, the largest part of which is grown in Dorchester and Wicomico Counties on the Eastern Shore. Maryland ranked first among the states of the United States last year in the total pack of whole tomatoes. Field hands pick the vegetables, pack them in baskets and they are trucked to the canneries which operate in the tomato belt. They are Maryland's leading vegetable crop.

FOOLING THE DUCKS . . . The Chesapeake Bay and the Susquehanna flats provide excellent duck hunting because the entire area is along the migration route of many species of ducks. Havre de Grace is the center of the canvasback country and is the home of this maker of decoys. Eleven different varieties of decoys are made and pride is taken in getting the colors just right. Of the ducks, the canvasback is the acknowledged king. Some waterfowl, such as the coot and scoter, are known as "trash ducks" and it is said that the best way to cook them is to nail them to an old locust board, bake in the oven for five hours and then throw the carcasses away and eat the board. Below are shown duck hunters in a blind in Talbot County.

THIRD HAVEN MEETING HOUSE . . . In Easton, at the south end of Washington Street, is the Third Haven Meeting House, the oldest frame house of worship in the United States, built by the Quakers in 1682-83. Both the building and the records of the meetings have been carefully preserved. William Penn was a visitor to this spot around which grew a small community. The town became Talbot County Courthouse, and in 1789, its name was changed to Easton, which it bears to the present day.

ANDERTON . . . It's better to stoop than pay taxes—or at least so the builder of this "skull buster" house believed in 1660 when it was erected. In those days the amount of taxes on a property was determined by the height of the eaves from the ground, so the story goes, and to keep the eaves near the earth it was necessary to pitch the roof sharply and make the doorway low. This doorway to the outside is only four feet in height and the ten inside doors are five feet, eight inches. This is probably one of the most interesting houses in Maryland awaiting restoration. It is located near Easton, Talbot County.

OTWELL, TALBOT COUNTY (above) . . . The gambrel-roofed sections were erected in 1670 of vari-colored brick burnt on the property. Other sections were added later. Below: CLARK'S CONVENIENCY. Built by Dennis Clark in 1707. This beautiful home is situated on Quaker Neck, near Chestertown.

WYE HOUSE . . . Talbot County. This is the finest wooden Colonial home in Maryland and dates from 1780 although the Lloyd family had settled the land as early as 1661. Lloyd descendants still occupy the house. Behind the house are formal gardens which contain box hedges over 200 years old. Three miles of walks are in the gardens and in the midst of these is the famous Orangery where citrus fruits were grown and which antedates the house itself. Nine generations of Lloyds are buried in the graveyard.

SHE LEANS . . . This picturesque ruin is on Kent Island in Queen Annes County. It is near the former Romancoke ferry terminal and overlooks Eastern Bay. While some of the state's old structures are dilapidated and in need of repairs, there are many others whose owners have either kept them in condition over the years or have restored them to their former beauty. There is much of Colonial America in Maryland.

WYE OAK . . . In Talbot County stands the Maryland state tree, a white oak so huge as to be almost beyond belief. It is the largest white oak in the nation, with a circumference of fifty-eight feet and a height of ninety-five feet. Its tremendous branches, some of which are as large as an ordinary tree, spread one hundred and sixty-five feet. The tree is estimated to be at least four hundred years old.

LITTLE WHITE SCHOOLHOUSE . . . Closed years ago when a fine, new consolidated school was opened in Preston, Caroline County, this little schoolhouse still remains near the town. To reach it you need only drive out of Easton on Dover Street and just east of the Dover bridge go south on Tanyard Road for a mile. The area was originally settled by a migration of Dutch settlers who founded a small town there in 1897.

REID HALL . . . This is one of ten fine buildings which may be seen on the campus of Washington College at Chestertown, Kent County. This was the first college to bear the name of George Washington; the Maryland legislature in 1782 passed an act founding the school ". . . in honorable and perpetual memory of George Washington." The first commencement was held in 1783 when six scholars graduated and in 1789 the college conferred an honorary degree of Doctor of Laws on its namesake. The first building burned in 1827. The college was founded by the Reverend William Smith.

MARYLAND IN MENU . . . "America in Miniature" applies to the food of Maryland as well as the topography of the state itself. Perhaps no other state is blessed with such an abundance and wide variety of foods—wild ducks and geese, deer, oysters, crabs, grouse, turkeys, and the famous diamond-backed terrapin. No matter where you travel you will find "Maryland" Fried Chicken, "Maryland" this and "Maryland" that on the menus, for the state has been a gourmet's paradise since Colonial days.

*Maryland Fried Chicken*

Cut up a young, tender chicken. Dredge with flour, then fry in deep fat to a golden brown. Serve on a layer of fried cornmeal mush or johnnycake with cream gravy poured over the cornbread.

Beaten biscuits are perhaps the oddest item of cookery to be found in the state. Not only are the right ingredients needed but a good right arm as well, for the dough is beaten with an ax for thirty minutes! Here's the recipe if you'd like to try it:

*Maryland Beaten Biscuits*

1/2 pint of flour
1/3 teaspoon lard
1/3 teaspoon salt.

Sift salt into flour. Rub lard in thoroughly and add a mixture of half milk and half water to make a very stiff dough. Knead for five minutes then beat with an ax for a half hour, or more! Shape into biscuits, prick tops and bake in moderate oven twenty minutes.

Perhaps the most famous item on the Maryland menus is the diamond-back terrapin, which was once so common in the bay that a law was passed which prohibited slave owners from feeding it to their slaves more than once a week. This delicacy is now so scarce that the turtles bring a minimum of several dollars each and a serving of diamond-back in a restaurant costs a small ransom. Fortunately the turtle is staging a comeback through wise conservation measures.

SEA FOOD CAPITAL . . . Such is Crisfield in Somerset County. It is Maryland's most southerly city, jutting out on a spit of land toward Tangier Sound. The houses scattered among the old piers and the packing plants are a photographer's paradise. Many of the old stores have false upper fronts, such as were found in western towns during the gold rush. Nearly all of the houses and docks are built on millions of bushels of oyster shells placed there before the state required a percentage of them to be used for replanting. Sailboats are present, but in ever decreasing numbers as powerboats take over. The town calls itself the seafood capital of the world, and one will agree after visiting the vast expanse of crab floats and busy packing houses.

WIND ALOFT . . . The Chesapeake is Maryland's greatest natural resource with over 3600 miles of shoreline in the state. The tiny rivers and creeks which creep inland from the bay provide a source of wonderful names: Sassafras, Bohemia, Patuxent, Nanticoke, Annemessex, Choptank, Pocomoke and Wicomico. There is a Wicomico River on each side of the bay.

# The Bay

BLOODY POINT LIGHT . . . This is one of the major lights in the bay. It is off the tip of Kent Island on the shelf of the main channel and takes its name from the area at the end of the island. Three ancient accounts, all different, offer the reason for the name "Bloody Point." One claims a massacre of Indians by the whites, another a fight during the Claiborne rebellion and the last the hanging of a French pirate.

SCHOONERS AND SKIPJACK . . . Typical bay boats are these three. At the right is the skipjack Esther W., which was built in 1914. The skipjack is usually a small vessel with a pronounced rake to the mast, a large jib, a triangular mainsail and a low freeboard. In the center is the schooner Mattie F. Dean, built in 1884 at Madison, Maryland. At the left is the schooner Anna and Helen, which was built in 1911. The boats are working the oyster beds off Matapeake.

LOG CANOE . . . This type of boat is modeled after those used by the Indians in Maryland waters, who cut boats from a single log. The modern canoe is made from several logs to attain greater size. Today they are used only for racing and as early as 1859 there were organized regattas held on the Eastern Shore. The boat in the picture is the Valiant Lady, formerly the Adelaide, which was built at Kent Island 85 years ago and is still being used in racing. The springboard when loaded with a crewman or two keeps the boat balanced.

Schooners and Skipjack

WING AND WING . . . Log canoes with all canvas set are a beautiful sight. These six were racing in the Miles River Regatta. Originally these boats were intended as work boats but their owners put on more and more sail to increase their speed until they became racing and pleasure craft only.

BUGEYE CATHERINE . . . A bugeye is a two-master, which is characterized by a sharp bow and stern. Actually it is a larger development of the original Indian log canoe. The origin of the name is widely speculated upon by lovers of sailing craft. The most widely accepted story is that, viewed head on, the holes for the anchor chains reminded someone long ago of "bug's eyes." The name caught the popular fancy and the boats have been called that ever since.

NO POWER . . . Because the boats which work the oyster beds must be without power, they carry a small motorboat on davits at the stern. If becalmed, the captain puts the small boat in the water and, starting the engine, lets it push the sailboat back to dock. The fact that all oyster dredging must be done under sail is in no small measure responsible for the preservation of sailboats on the bay. This is the Thomas Clyde.

OYSTER DREDGERS ON THE CHOPTANK . . . This is the picture that won a five thousand dollar prize in a contest sponsored by *Photography* magazine. It shows the skipjacks Maggie Lee and Lucy Tyler in a driving rain, in which the crew continued to work. They seem oblivious of the weather. Evidence of the intensity of the storm can be found by looking closely at the water, the black spots having been caused by the rain actually knocking holes into the Choptank as it fell. This picture has had a great success in photographic exhibitions at home and abroad, for it has feeling, mood, and dramatic values of high caliber.

DEXTROUS FLEET . . . When dredging oysters the boats work back and forth over the bar, scraping the oysters off the bottom with dredges. These are raised periodically by a small donkey engine located amidships, the only source of power permitted on the boats. The skippers judge the wind and water so well that they can work in close quarters that would frighten an ordinary motorist were the bay a roadway. As any sailor knows, it is difficult to jockey a sailboat in ordinary weather; these oystermen do it in fair or foul.

PAYING OFF . . . Filling the sails with wind and gathering headway is known as "paying off." This boat captain holds a control rope to the donkey engine in each hand, which leaves only a foot with which to steer the boat among all the other boats working the bar. Oystermen refer to their boats as "drudge" boats.

THE MOST DIFFICULT JOB IN THE WORLD . . . Tonging oysters by hand from the bay bottom is tough, cold, rugged work. Men go out in small boats with rakes on the ends of handles which sometimes measure twenty-four feet in length. Most of the tonging is done in the cold weather when ice frequently forms on the handles. The teeth of the rake scrape the oysters off the bottom. Special areas are set aside for the hand tongers; dredgers are not allowed there. If either finds the other infringing an argument ensues.

BUY BOAT . . . The buy boats work among the fleet, taking off the oysters and running them to the packing houses. Careful watch is kept of the number of baskets swung aboard and the oysterman keeps a tally also. If the two do not agree, the bickering begins. All oysters must be over three inches in length; smaller ones must be dropped back in the bay. The state maintains a fleet of patrol boats to watch the watermen.

HOME FROM THE BAY . . . When the oyster season closes, much of the fleet puts into Cambridge, one of the Eastern Shore's largest towns, just off the Choptank River. It is no longer feasible to use these boats for transportation as in the old days, as the Maryland conservation laws forbid any dredge boat to install power. Thus by good fortune, these picturesque craft still exist while the cargo sailboats have vanished.

SHELL SHEDDERS . . . In the crab floats at Crisfield a close watch is maintained to spot the instant a crab shucks off his old shell. The nearby Pocomoke and Tangier Sound provide a plentiful supply of hard crabs. During the shedding the crabs are known by the stages they are in. The first stage is a "green peeler," the second stage a "peeler," the third stage a "buster" and the final stage a soft crab—that's when the crab goes to market.

BAY HARVEST . . . During the spring shad and herring runs the commercial fishermen have an exciting time. The shad, and especially its roe, is a real Maryland delicacy. After this great migration period, the rockfish and hardheads follow, giving the sport fisherman lots of fun. The 180-mile long Chesapeake tops the world in seafood production for any bay of like size. From its depths come fish, crabs, oysters and terrapin.

ALL METHODISTS . . . Smith Island, which lies in the bay off Crisfield, has four distinctions. It has seldom been known to cast a single Democratic vote, the people are all devout Methodists and the island is the most southerly of the state's possessions and the largest island in the bay. There is an abundance of wildlife, which the people consider to be theirs by the grace of God—game wardens stay away. The island was founded by Captain John Smith of Pocohontas fame. The "main street" is about ten feet wide. To visit it you must either hire a boat at Crisfield or go over on the mailboat, which makes the trip once a day. Cameras are not welcome on the island.

HOOPER ISLANDS . . . Situated in one of the greatest concentration areas for wild ducks and geese in the United States, the Hooper Islands are a hunter's paradise. So many birds fly about that it is necessary to put iron bars across the larger windows to prevent them from being broken, so islanders say. There are three islands, Upper, Middle and Lower. The first mentioned are inhabited but the last is a retreat for hunters.

CHESAPEAKE BAY BRIDGE . . . History was made on July 30, 1952, when Maryland's Eastern and Western Shores at last were linked—after years of discussion and planning—by the largest all-over-water steel bridge in the world. The great structure measures 4.35 miles from shore to shore, and 7.72 miles overall. It cost $44,000,000. A panoramic picture of it appears on the cover of this book.

CHESAPEAKE BAY BRIDGE

O'er the Ramparts

O'ER THE RAMPARTS... Fort McHenry at the mouth of Baltimore's inner harbor is the site of the birth of "The Star-Spangled Banner." Francis Scott Key on the ship Minden, watched the battle on September 13, 1814. Rockets were used during the bombardment of the fort and on the next morning Key observed that the flag was still there. The battle was spectacular but did little damage. The guns now to be seen at the fort were not used then; they are Civil War weapons. There are, incidentally, only two places in Maryland where the American flag flies both day and night—Fort McHenry, and Key's grave in Frederick.

ABANDONED FORT... Brevet Colonel Robert E. Lee, at that time an engineer in the U. S. Army, supervised the building of Fort Carroll on a man-made island in the center of the Patapsco River in 1848. Although it was intended that the fort would be a full military post, it was never completed. Today it is merely a menace to navigation, although its stout walls are well-equipped with all sorts of warning devices. Lee had no way of knowing that a scant fifteen years later he would be leading a fight against the North and that thousands of his men would be imprisoned at Fort McHenry, a few miles away from Fort Carroll.

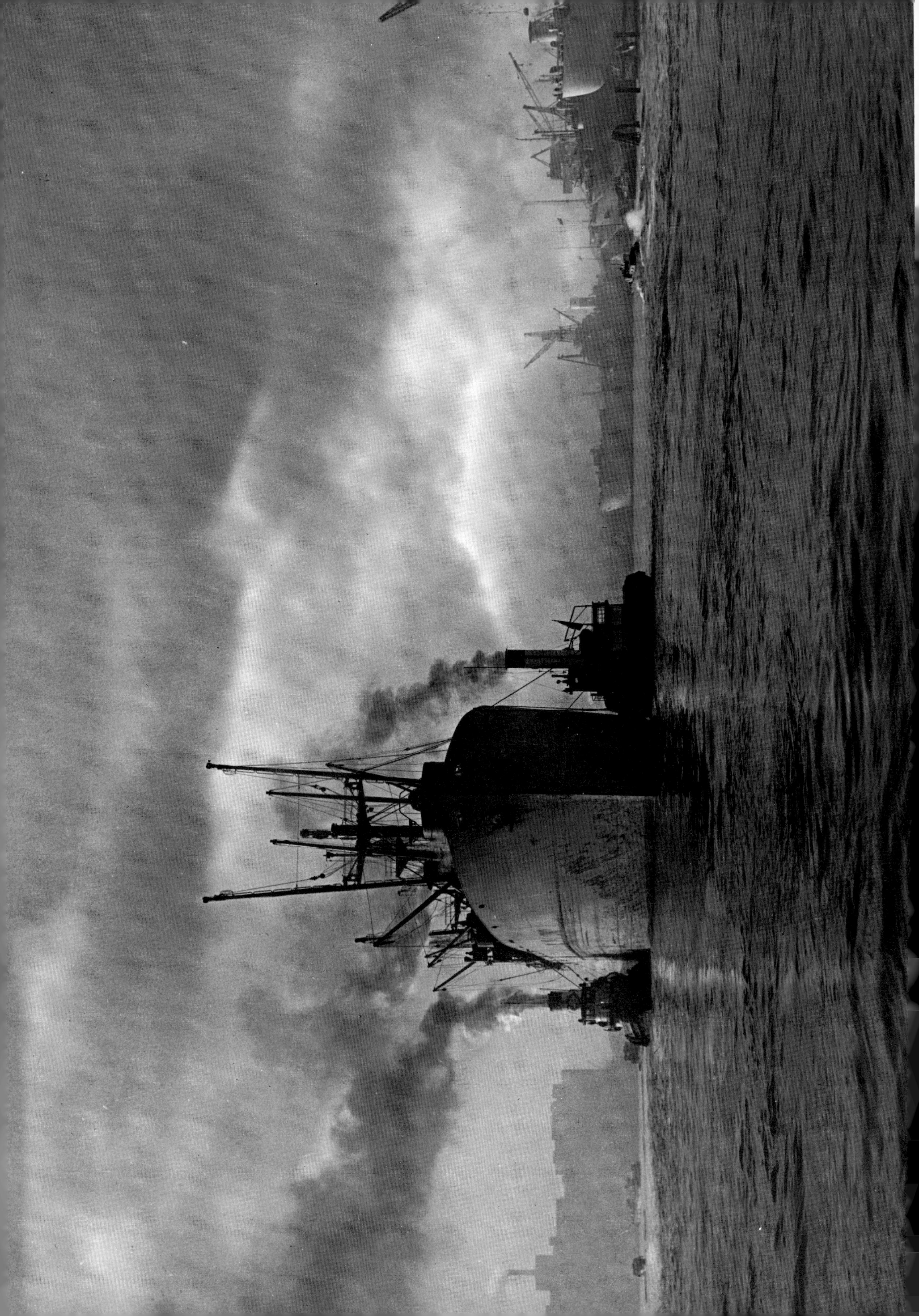

BALTIMORE HARBOR . . . Forty-six miles of waterfront bustles with the varied traffic that makes Baltimore the nation's second seaport in total volume of foreign commerce. As the tugs work the huge freighter up the harbor past the sugar refinery on the left and the Bethlehem ship repair yard on the right it seems a far cry from the early days of the privateers and the swift Baltimore clippers that made the name of the city feared and respected. Since Colonial days, Baltimore has been an important port.

SHIP TO TRAIN . . . Framed by the girders of a huge pier crane is the La Salle, one of the modern ships calling at Port Covington, Baltimore, the tidewater terminal of the Western Maryland Railway Company, where the trains run down to the dockside. The hold of this giant of the seas could carry the cargo of a dozen clipper ships that made Baltimore famous in the early days. The first clipper in the China trade was the Ann McKim. Many of these craft were used during the War of 1812 to harass the large British ships.

ICE BREAKER . . . In more ways than one the ship Latrobe is an ice breaker. In the winter she keeps the harbor channel open and in the warm months serves as a good-will boat, taking convention visitors and children for tours. Built in 1879, this sidewheeler is the oldest large boat in the harbor, if not the bay.

THE CALVERT . . . This vessel is screw propelled and formerly operated in the Potomac, Rappahannock, Tred Avon and Choptank Rivers. During World War II she served with distinction in the U. S. Navy.

NARROW BEAM . . . The Anthony Groves, Jr.· (upper right) was built in 1893 and is screw propelled. Her beam is only twenty-three feet to allow her to pass through the locks of the Chesapeake and Delaware Canal. She no longer operates.

WASHINGTON RUN . . . The Talbot, a steel hulled sidewheeler, was built at Sparrows Point in 1912 and after operating in the Tred Avon and Choptank was put on the Washington D. C. run. Washington to Baltimore, airline, is only 40 miles but by water it is 320 miles. The trip took about 36 hours.

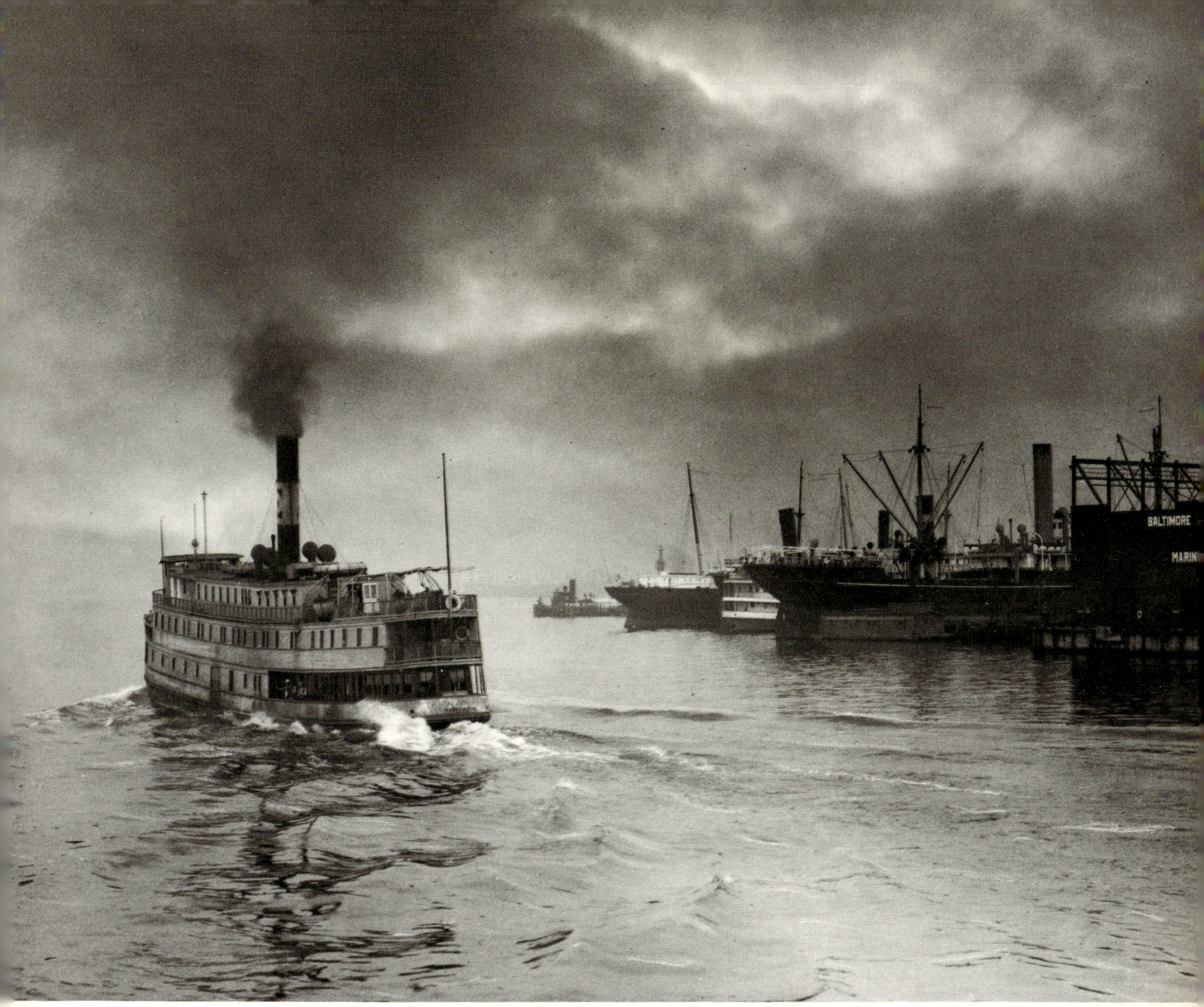
BALTIMORE

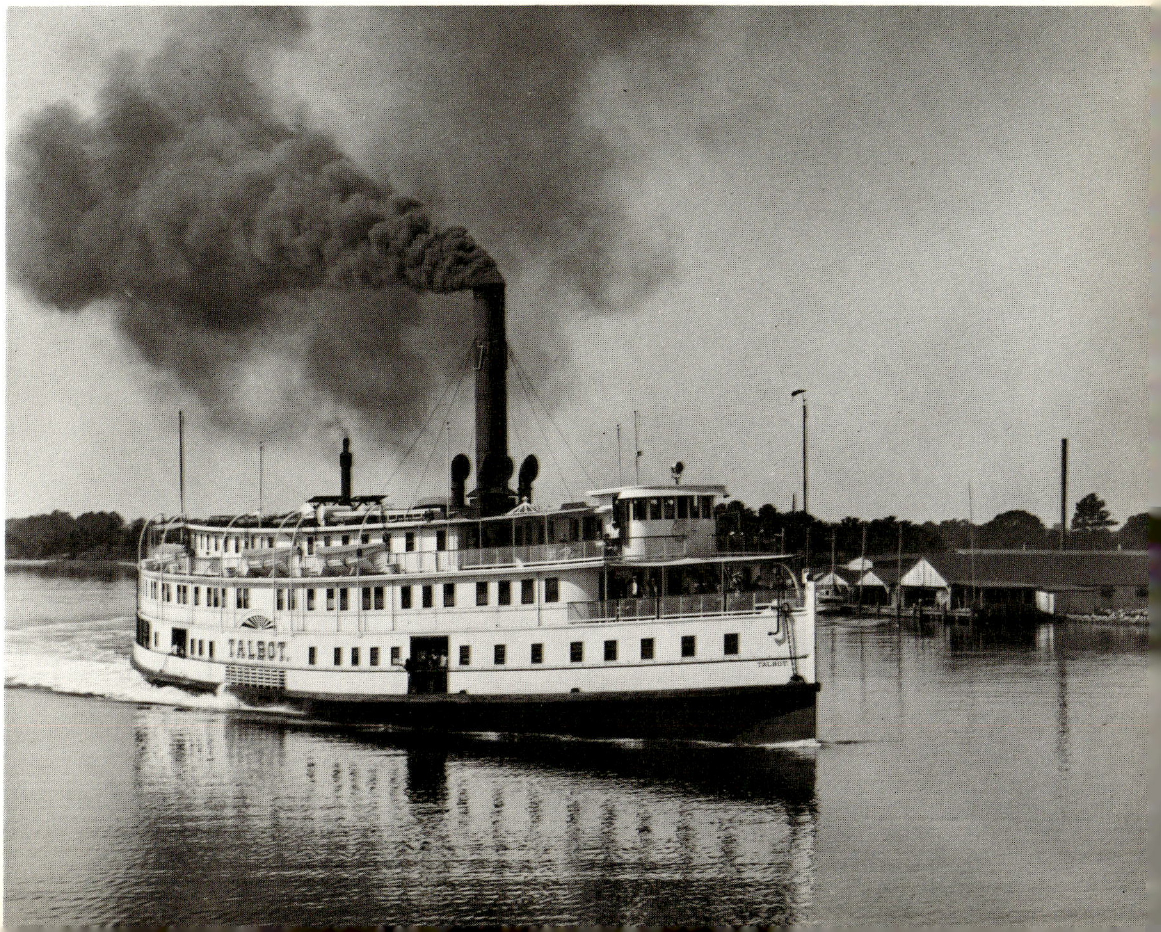
TALBOT

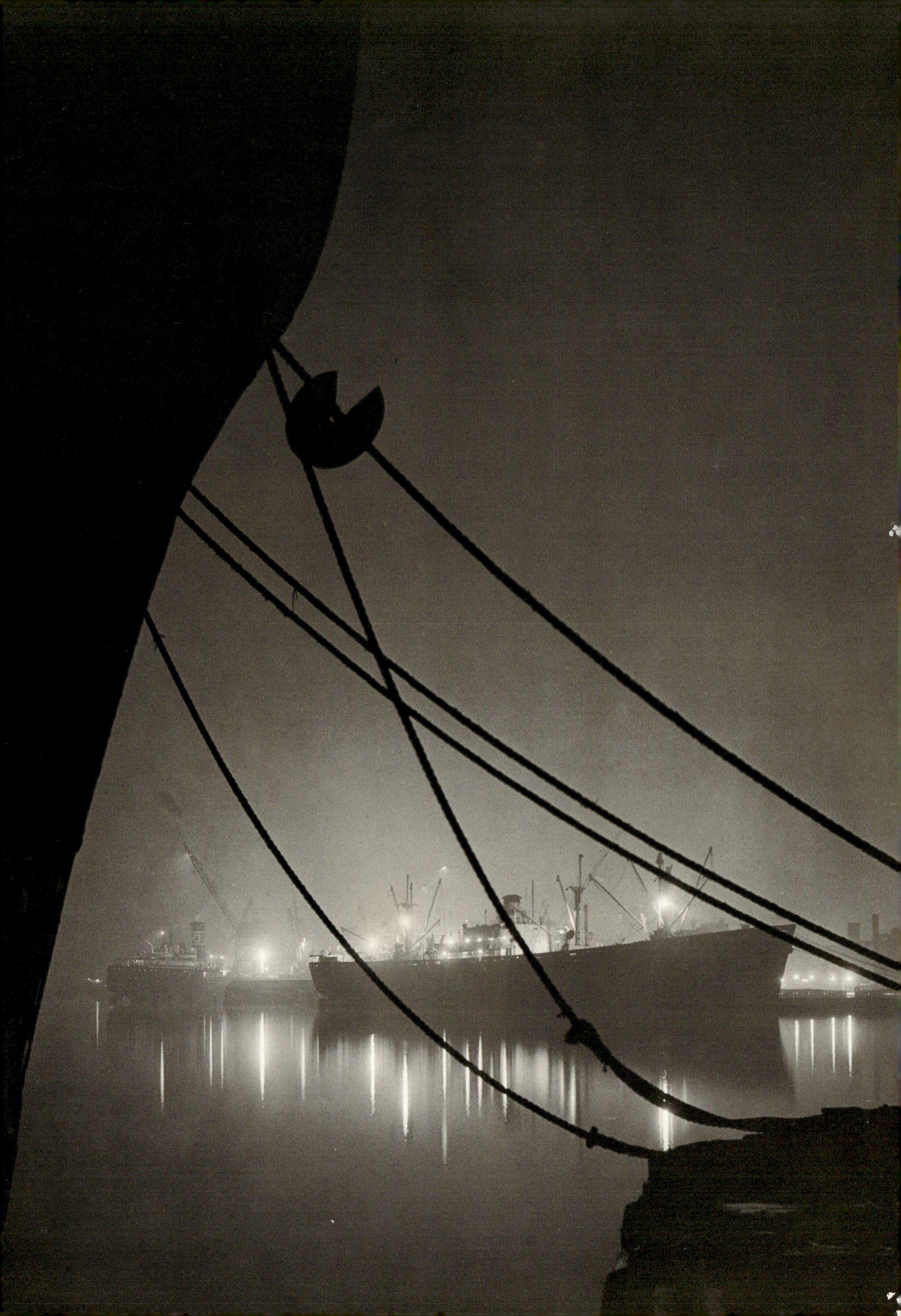

DAY, NIGHT, WINTER, SUMMER . . . In the old days the sailing boats hove into Baltimore with cargoes of melons and tomatoes and anchored at Long Dock. This was one trip the baymen enjoyed for it gave them the opportunity to visit the ship chandlers, sail lofts, taverns, rooming houses—and just plain joints.

# Baltimore—1729

Two and a quarter centuries after their founding, some Maryland settlements have disappeared entirely, some remain small and quaint and flavorous of those days long gone, some others have grown moderately. But Baltimore, since 1729, has forged its way high up in the ranks of the nation's great cities and today presents to the eye, and the imagination, an endless array of colorful and contrasting facets.

Bright facets, too; so bright that many a one is sufficient in itself to hold the gaze. Thus some beholders see only the vast and throbbing world port, others only the hallowed patriotic shrine, the world-renowned medical and educational center, or the museums and schools devoted to the fine arts, and so on. Still others, limited to a quick glance, remember the city ever afterward for its famous rows of gleaming white steps, or the countless statues and other monuments that dot its streets and parks and bring it the nickname of Monumental City.

All of these facets catch the eye of the photographer, too, and all are represented on the pages that follow. But as he explores the city's odd corners and byways, the photographer comes upon many things that are less conspicuous, but no less interesting and no less characteristic of his Baltimore. And so pictures of these things, too, will be found.

There are, for instance, some steps that should be as famous as the white ones—the wooden steps of Fountain Street that are turned upside down, or even taken indoors, when the home-owner wishes to discourage callers. There are such picturesque scenes as Tyson Street on a snowy night, and that created by a house at Elliott and Streeper Streets that is simply covered with elaborate grillwork. All details in the great panorama of present-day Baltimore, but all fascinating details of—My Baltimore.

CUBIST DESIGN . . . The row after row of white steps for which the city is famous form the basis for this photographic design. If you can't figure it out, turn the book to the right and the steps may be plainly seen.

WASHINGTON MONUMENT . . . This imposing Doric column was designed by Robert Mills in 1809 but was not completed until November 20, 1829. Funds for its erection were raised by lottery and some were obtained from the state but the money ran out and the War of 1812 halted progress on the monument. It was the first monument begun in the honor of George Washington but not the first to be completed for the town of Boonsboro in Washington County put up a rough stone monument in one day on July 4, 1827.

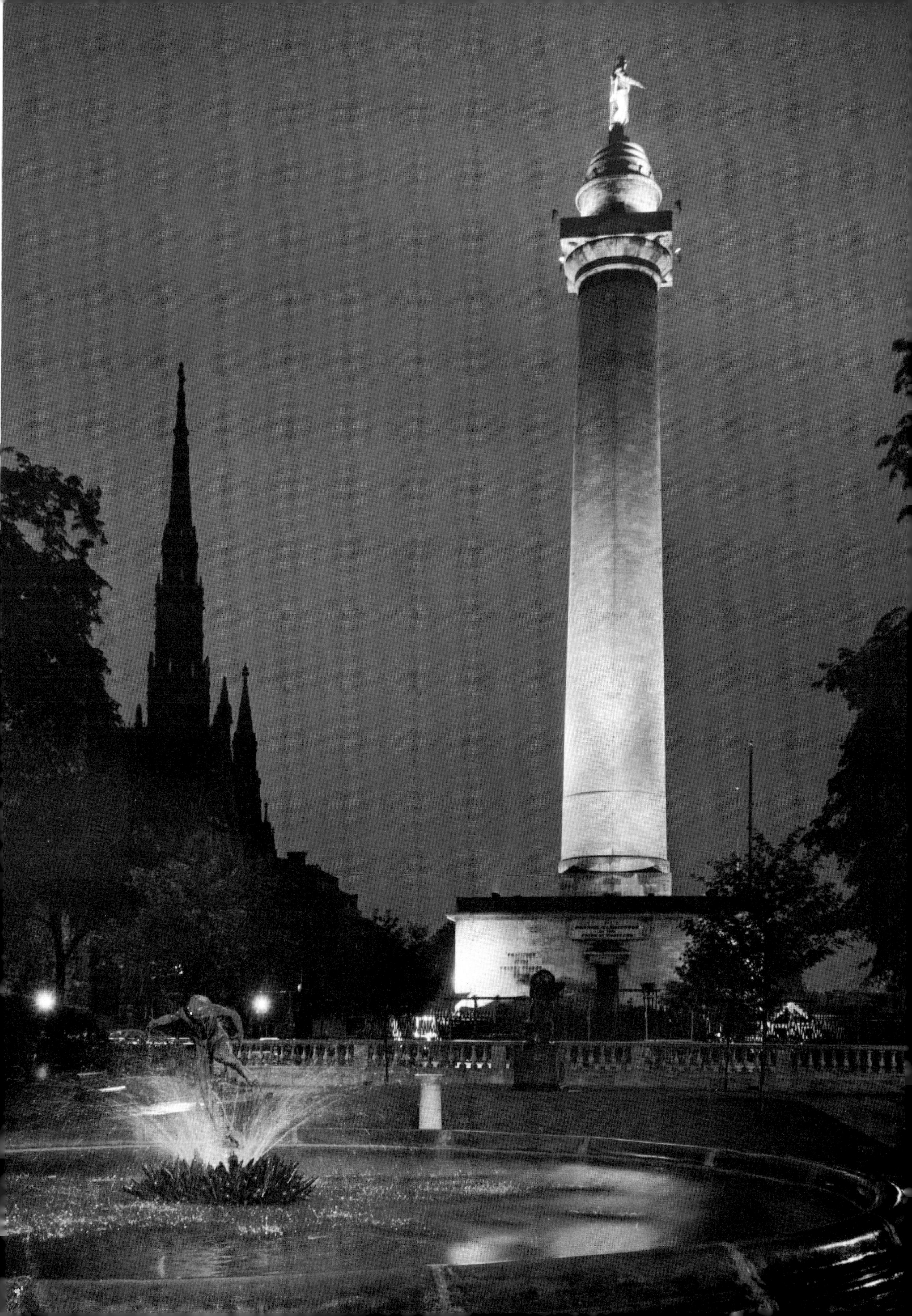

BALTIMORE BY DAY... As seen from Federal Hill, which is across the harbor from the business district, the Monumental City presents this imposing appearance. Highest of the structures is the Mathieson Building, atop which is the modern batwing antenna of television station WMAR-TV. Piers line the far shore.

BALTIMORE BY NIGHT . . . After the sun has set the city presents this view from the same vantage point of Federal Hill, which is a city park. The hill has a colorful history. In 1797 a lookout tower was built on it to give advance notice to the Maritime Exchange of ships entering the harbor.

GUESS WHICH . . . The 2600 block of Wilkens Avenue is one of the longest unbroken blocks in the city. Fifty-four houses long, those toward the end bear half-numbers. It is a wise owner who knows his own steps and can enter the house without checking the number.

STEPS—AND STEPS . . . The white steps of Baltimore have become the city's trademark and a marvel to visitors. Most of them are white marble, from nearby quarries, and housewives vie in keeping them bright. In any block, there is seldom a day that someone is not out scrubbing them. On the older houses, the scraping of countless thousands of footsteps has worn grooves in the stone.

ODDEST STEPS . . . Down in Fells Point, on Fountain Street, and on nearby Shakespeare Street, where Fell, the founder of the section, lies buried, are these odd—and practical—steps. If the householder does not wish to be disturbed by callers or peddlers he turns his steps up or takes them indoors. Entrance to the houses is mostly through the kitchen, which is reached by the walkway between the houses.

INDUSTRY. THE BETHLEHEM STEEL COMPANY PLANT AT SPARROWS POINT

ONE OF MANY . . . The statues and other sculptured memorials that fill her streets and parks long ago gained for Baltimore the nickname Monumental City. This imposing example of the works pays tribute to Robert E. Lee and Stonewall Jackson. It stands in Wyman Park, opposite the Museum of Art.

THE POE HOUSE . . . Edgar Allan Poe courted his cousin in this house at 203 Amity Street. She was Virginia Clemm, who later became his wife. During a slum clearance project the house was slated to be razed but Poe admirers protested, saved the house and restored it, furnishing it with many of the original items.

MOUNT CLARE STATION . . . This is the first railroad passenger and freight station to be erected in the United States. It was built on land deeded to the railroad by Charles Carroll of Carrollton. In May 1830, the first trip over the new roadbed was made to Ellicott's Mills, using a horse to draw the train. The first American-built steam locomotive, Tom Thumb, was built by Peter Cooper in a shop near the station. On May 24, 1844 the world's first official telegraph message was received at the station from Samuel F. B. Morse in Washington. The roundhouse behind it is one of the largest and most interesting in existence.

ORNAMENTAL IRON . . . The grillwork on some of the older buildings is magnificently done, as on this house at Elliott and Streeper Streets near Fells Point. Many of the old homes in this section have beautiful examples rivaling those of New Orleans.

ORNAMENTAL IRON

SHERWOOD GARDENS . . . This privately owned garden covers seven acres and among its hundreds of kinds of spring blooming plants are 150,000 tulips imported from Holland. The garden is opened to the public every spring and on a good Sunday the attendance tops forty thousand persons.

SHOT TOWER . . . Almost a unique structure; there is one other in the United States. It was used to make shot. Molten lead was poured through a sieve at the top and it hardened into pellets as it fell. The tower is 234 feet tall and contains 1,100,000 bricks. It produced 12,500,000 pounds of shot during a year.

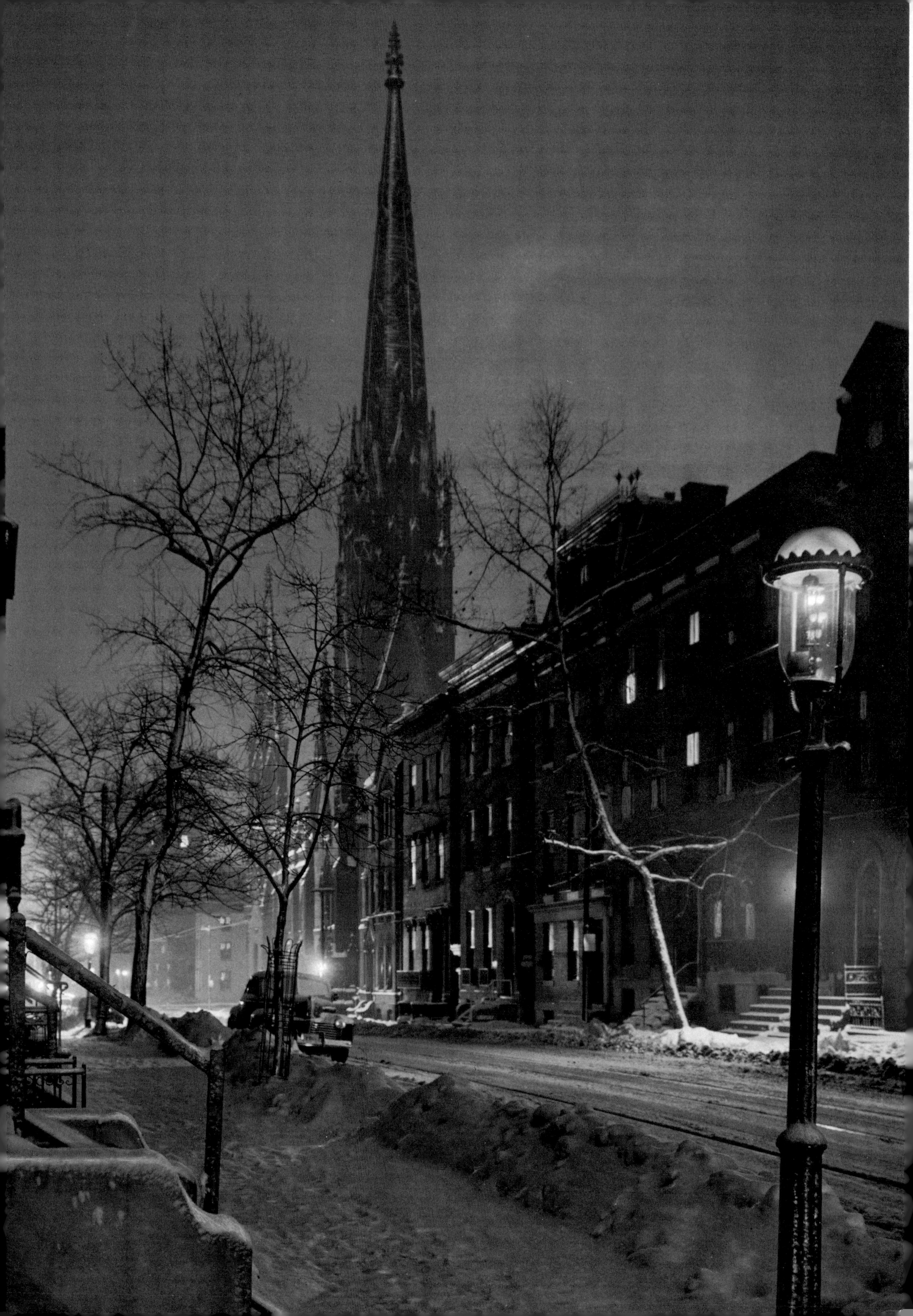

PARK AVENUE; NIGHT . . . On the corner of Park and Madison stands the magnificent First Presbyterian Church with its 273 foot high stone spire, considered to be one of the finest Gothic spires in America. For a time a tree sprouted from the stonework about a hundred feet above the ground, the seed doubtless dropped there by a bird. This is the fourth church building of the congregation, formed in 1761.

HOUSE PATTERN . . . During World War II there was a steady influx of new workers into Baltimore to man the many war industries, and housing developments such as this sprang up almost overnight. This one at nearby Dundalk forms an excellent pattern-picture subject when seen from an airplane. The curving layout of the streets and the repetition of the houses make it interesting.

THE CATHEDRAL . . . The Cathedral of the Assumption of the Blessed Virgin Mary was the first Roman Catholic cathedral in the United States. Its cornerstone was laid in 1806; at that time more than half of the Catholics in the nation lived in Maryland. On Palm Sunday in 1942—the date was March 29—an unprecedented twenty-two inch snow blanketed the city. This picture of the Cathedral was made on that day.

WASHINGTON PLACE . . . Looking south on Charles Street, the Walters Art Gallery can be seen at right. The famous Peabody Conservatory of Music is to the left of this garden spot.

SHAAREI TFILOH SYNAGOGUE . . . This beautiful Romanesque building, designed by Stanislaus Russell, was dedicated in 1921; not until some years later, however, was it raised to the full height of its coppered dome. Here it is shown through a frame of trees in Druid Hill Park, west of which it stands.

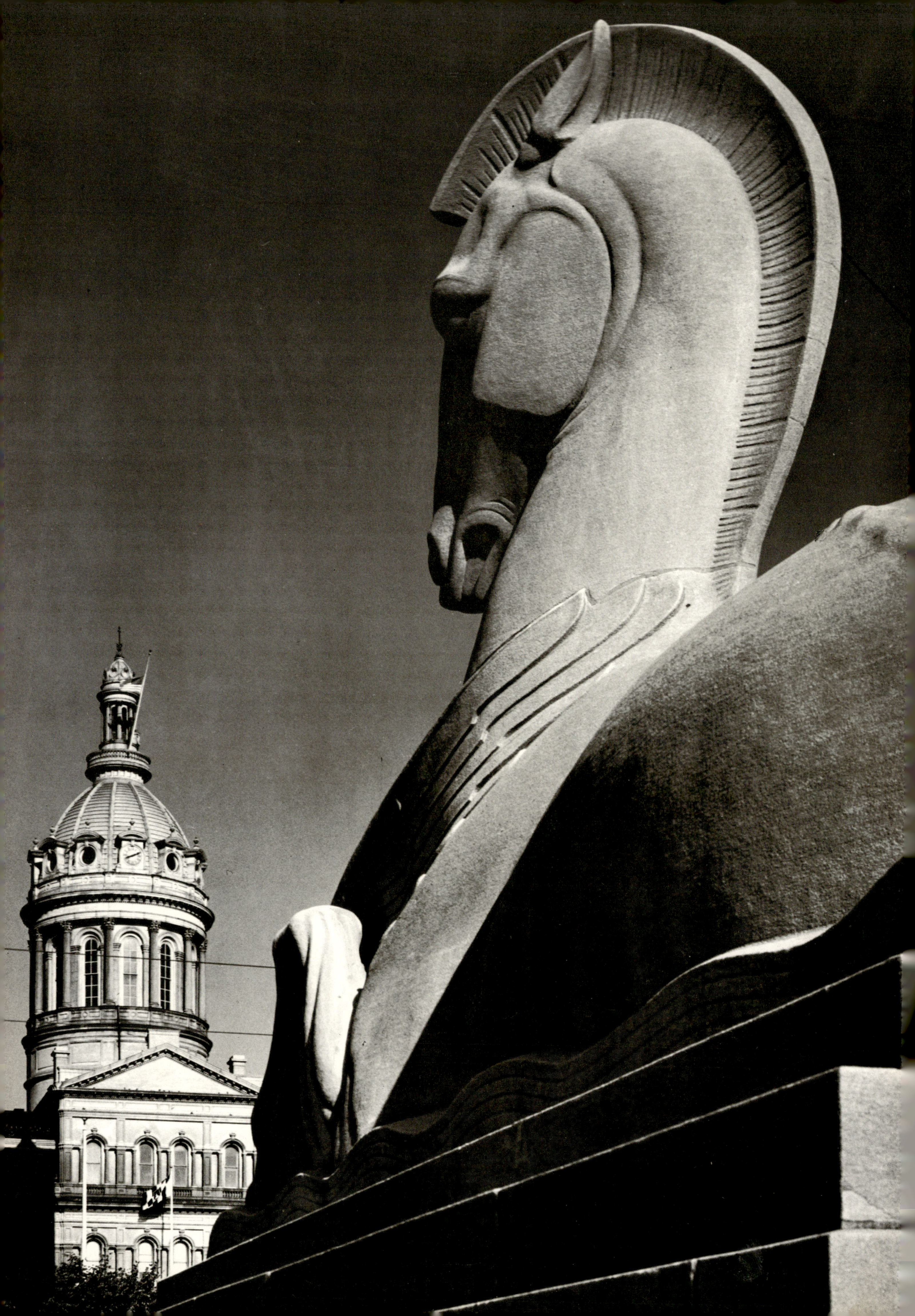

CITY HALL . . . The Baltimore City Hall may be unique as a civic edifice—it was constructed and furnished for less money than had been appropriated for the purpose. The building is of Baltimore County marble and has a cast iron dome. In the foreground is one of the horses which flank the entrance to the War Memorial.

PRATT LIBRARY . . . Ranking high among public libraries of the world is the Enoch Pratt Free Library. It was opened in 1884 to serve "all citizens, regardless of property or color." The donor was Enoch Pratt, an enterprising Yankee merchant who migrated to Maryland in 1831. This central building is regarded as a model library structure and has been widely copied. There are twenty-seven branches, built with Carnegie funds, and two bookmobiles. All of these together circulate over three million books a year. In addition, the library is a willing information bureau, answering an average of almost a half-million queries a year on all sorts of topics.

AIR CASTLES . . . On Madison Street, looking toward Charles, are these distinguished homes reflecting the older city. Many of the buildings have been converted to apartments but the feeling of the area is still one of quiet and dignity.

FRANCIS SCOTT KEY MONUMENT . . . At Eutaw Place and Lanvale is this monument to the writer of "The Star-Spangled Banner." It shows Key offering his manuscript to Columbia. The original MS. is in the Walters Art Gallery. Recently some "Tory" proposed that the city raze the monument, complaining that mosquitoes were breeding in the rain-filled boat! The Columbus monument on the facing page is an obelisk built of cemented brick and was dedicated in 1792. It was the first monument erected to honor Columbus in the New World and it still is unknown to most Baltimoreans.

OLD SAINT PAUL'S GRAVEYARD . . . In this graveyard are buried many of the heroes of Baltimore's long history including Colonel John Eager Howard, distinguished Revolutionary War soldier, Colonel George Armistead, who commanded Fort McHenry, and Charles Carroll, the barrister. Dating back to 1800, it is the oldest and most historic graveyard in the city. In the background is the University of Maryland Hospital, a 12-story brick and limestone building erected in 1934. Alongside are the Medical and Law and Dental Schools. The latter school has George Washington's false teeth.

First Monument to Columbus, 1792

HOMEWOOD . . . On the campus of Johns Hopkins University is this splendid example of Georgian architecture, which followed the Colonial. It is a five-part house and unlike other early homes, is of one story. It was built by Charles Carroll of Carrollton for his son in 1809. It is now used for offices of the President of Johns Hopkins University.

MEDICINE . . . The Johns Hopkins Hospital—world-renowned center for patient care, medical education and scientific research—has patients, students and doctors present from all over the earth. It first received worldwide attention after the turn of the century through the efforts of the "Big Four"—Doctors Welch, Kelly, Osler and Halstead.

GILMAN HALL . . . Founded by a Baltimore merchant and opened in 1876, Hopkins was the first "true" university in America. Internationally famous for its contributions to science and the humanities, the school has long been a leader in training young men to carry out research in these areas of knowledge.

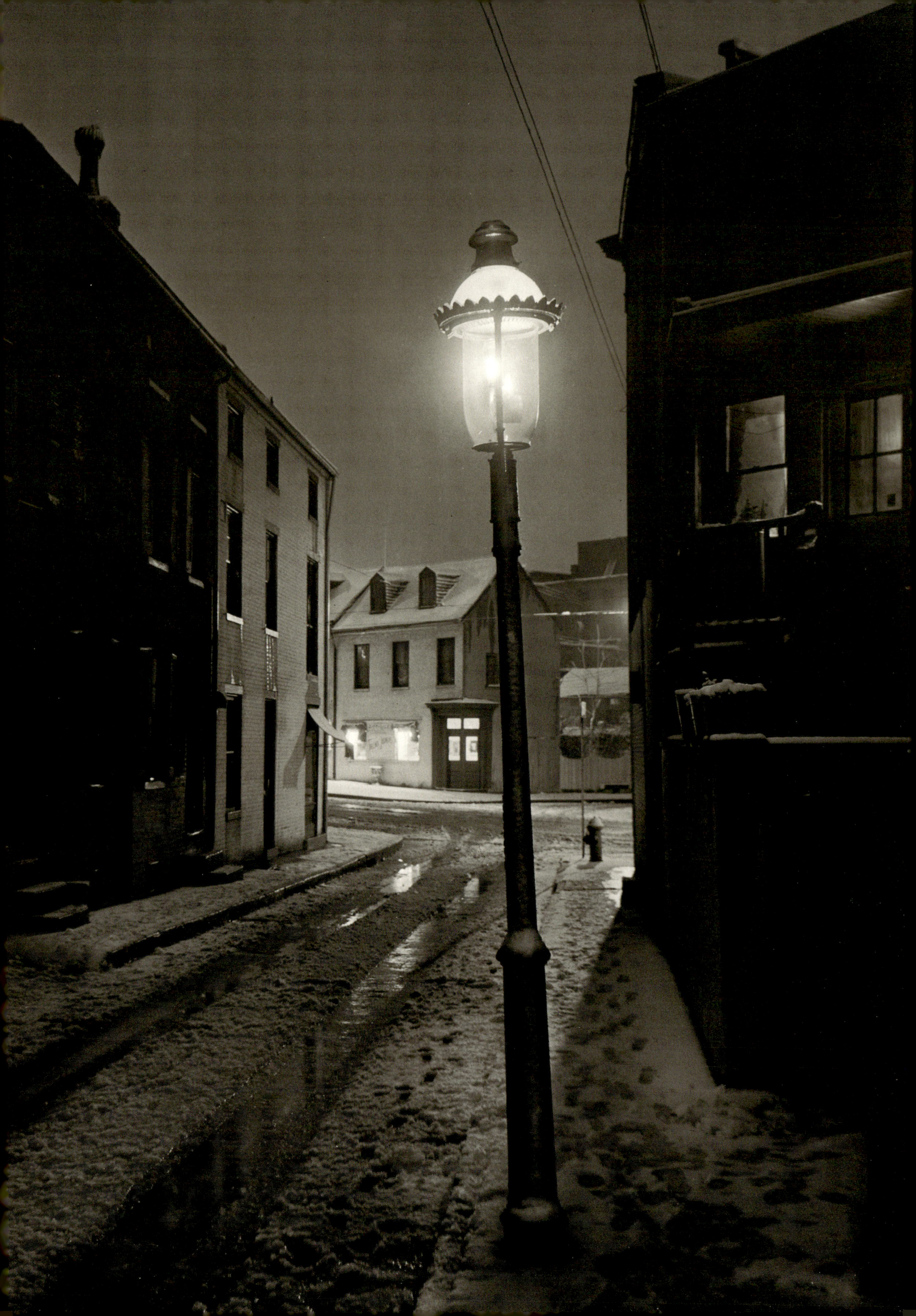

TYSON STREET AT NIGHT . . . This narrow street has been taken over and the buildings restored by an artistic group. Baltimore was the first city to be lighted by gas and today there are still almost thirteen thousand gas lamps in the city.

THE FLAG HOUSE . . . It was in this building that Mary Pickersgill sewed the Star-Spangled Banner that flew over Fort McHenry during the bombardment by the British. The flag was thirty by forty-two feet; it was made so large so that the sight of it would inspire the citizens to greater efforts.

AMERICA'S OLDEST MUSEUM . . . (right). In 1813, Rembrandt Peale, the famous American artist, erected this building on Holliday Street "for the sole purpose of . . . A Museum and Gallery for fine paintings," the first time this had been done in America. In 1816 he gave a demonstration of illuminating gas and helped found the Baltimore Gas Light Company, the first such company in the United States. From 1830 to 1875 the building served as Baltimore's City Hall and in 1931 it was restored and re-opened as The Peale Museum, devoted to the life and history of Baltimore.

OLD HILLTOP . . . Pimlico race track is world famous and is the home of such nationally known races as the Preakness, the Dixie and the Futurity. This picture was taken on Preakness Day. The Preakness was first run on May 27, 1873, and was named for a famous three-year-old. Pimlico was one of the first tracks to adopt the pari-mutuel system of betting, the totalisator and the starting gate. It is one of the few race courses which is entirely within the confines of a large city and on famous race days the attendance will go over the thirty thousand mark.

OVER A THOUSAND STALLS . . . The Lexington Market is a shopping center for Baltimore. To it, farmers bring delicacies, meats, vegetables, preserves and even mead, which is an effervescent drink made of honey. The old building shown here was burned down on March 25, 1949, and has been replaced with a most modern structure containing the best in food handling equipment. Despite the modernization, it still retains much of the old tradition. The building which burned dated back to 1803, making the market one of the oldest in the nation, and was a Baltimore landmark.

DROODLE PARK ... At least that is the way many Baltimoreans pronounce Druid Hill Park, a wooded, hilly tract of 675 acres that contains many lakes, of which the boat lake shown above is one. Incredible as it may seem, underneath a large park reservoir is a parcel of land subject to an irredeemable ground rent—the city must pay an annual rental to an estate for use of the ground. Much planning and development have gone into the park and many parts of it are beautifully landscaped. It boasts a fine zoo.

HURRY, MARYLAND . . . The town of Hurry, in St. Marys County gives no evidence of living up to its name, as the picture shows. But before anyone chuckles too hard, in Baltimore a High Street crosses a Low Street. A few other odd place names in the state include Hog's Skull, Tippity Wichity, Fiddlesburg, Jugtown, Frogtown, Accident, T.B., Detour, Basket Switch, Burnt Store, Hole-in-the-Wall, Bivalve, Catch Penny Corner, Pomonkey, Red House, and Rush.

THE GENTLE FOLK . . . Twelve years ago, some Amish migrated to St. Marys County in the Free State to follow their age-old practices and beliefs. They settled in the Newmarket area and at present there are fifty families clinging to their old customs. There is no electricity, and windmills are used to pump water; buggies take the place of the modern automobile. No buttons, just hooks and eyes. The county conducts a school especially for the Amish children.

THE GENTLE FOLK

SOTTERLEY... This home in St. Marys County, overlooking the Patuxent River, is one of the show places of Maryland's oldest county. It is early Georgian Colonial and has been restored by a sympathetic owner even to removing parts that had been added to the original structure by previous owners, and carefully restoring the original rooms after a long and careful study. The house was built in 1730 and still bears the date on a plaque on the cupola. In the garden is the Sotterley sun dial which has noted the passing of time since 1734. Many old Maryland mansions, especially on the Eastern Shore, have been bought by people with the intention of restoring them to their original condition. This frequently results in much very expensive tearing down and rebuilding but the results justify the effort, for the old homes are truly distinctive.

MULBERRY FIELDS . . . Built sometime between 1760 and 1770 by William Somerville, this house is as nearly original as any Colonial house in Maryland. It is of Georgian Colonial design and the red bricks, made on the farm, are laid in an all-header bond. The view of the river front is magnificent—a vista of three quarters of a mile from the house to the Potomac. The small house on the right was used in the silk industry that the early settlers tried to establish. Two lines of huge mulberry trees, which run from the house to the river, were doubtless those planted by the owners to supply food for the silk-worms. The attempts to establish the silk industry in America were doomed to failure because the high costs, even with slave labor, prevented the colonists from making a reasonable profit on their labors.

TOBACCO IN THE RAW . . . This rolling tobacco field at Chaneyville, Calvert County, is but a small part of Maryland's tobacco acreage. Last year forty million pounds of tobacco were raised in the five Southern Maryland counties of Anne Arundel, Calvert, Prince Georges, St. Marys and Charles. The average yield per acre is a thousand pounds. Maryland tobacco is used principally for cigarettes and is very desirable due to its quick burning properties. About three to four per cent of it is used in each cigarette.

TOBACCO IN FLOWER . . . While everyone has seen tobacco in smoking form, a great number of people have never seen it growing and still a greater number have never seen its flower, shown above.

FORTY MILES FROM WASHINGTON . . . On the Lower Bramleigh farm, in St. Marys County, within forty miles of the nation's capital, you will find tobacco still being planted, cultivated, hauled and cured as it was three hundred years ago—using oxen, the most primitive kind of draft animal, for power. Good in boggy land, oxen are also found in remote areas on the Eastern Shore, where they are used in logging operations. Gradually disappearing from the Maryland scene, ox yokes are becoming the objects of antique-hunter's search, used as lawn ornaments and in other ways.

MARYLAND'S FIRST TOWN . . . It was in a village purchased from the Indians that Lord Baltimore's first colonists established themselves in Maryland after their voyage from England on the ships Ark and Dove. The historic purchase was made on March 27, 1634; payment was in axes, hatchets, farm implements and cloth. The place was then renamed St. Marys—the Indians had called it Yaocomico—and made the capital of the province. By 1676 the colony was populous enough, and prosperous enough, to erect a statehouse there; a replica of that structure, built in 1934, is pictured here. St. Marys remained the capital until 1694, when government offices were moved to Annapolis. For a bit longer it flourished as county seat, then lost that status to Leonardtown. That was a death blow.

POUND NETTING FOR SHAD . . . Pound nets are placed in the bay to catch shad, one of the great bay delicacies. Some of the larger fish are being tagged in order to determine their movements in an effort to increase their numbers. Nets are used to catch herring, rock and other varieties of fish, also. This picture was made near Point No Point on the Chesapeake Bay.

HUNTING FOR RAILBIRDS . . . Every fall thousands of birds migrate to feed on the wild oats which grow in great abundance over the vast marshes on the Patuxent River. To shoot the birds, it is best to get an early start, even before the mists from the river have been cleared away by the rising sun. The tiny boats are poled through the tall wild oats.

79

STATEHOUSE FROM CHANCELLOR COURT

OLDEST STATE CAPITOL ... The State House in Annapolis is the oldest state capitol still in use. Actually it is the third state house to be built in Maryland's capital city; the first was erected in 1697. The present building dates from 1772 and has been the scene of many important events in American history. On December 23, 1783, George Washington resigned his commission in the Old Senate Chamber. Congress met there from November 1783 to June of 1784 and ratified the signing of the treaty of peace with England, which had been negotiated in Paris. The dome is of hand hewn wood held together with wooden pins.

GOVERNOR'S MANSION ... Annapolis was laid out as a seat of government prior to 1700. The Governor's Mansion is located between two famous Circles. State Circle contains the State House and Church Circle is the site of Saint Anne's Church, established before 1704 and rebuilt in 1859. Erected in 1866, the Governor's Mansion was remodeled in 1936 to make it conform more closely to some of the older buildings in town. Annapolis has more original Colonial buildings standing than any other city in the United States; many of them are occupied and maintained by descendants of the original families that built them.

CITY DOCK, ANNAPOLIS . . . Here the small oyster, fishing, and crab boats tie up after a day in the bay and nearby rivers. Fishing parties will also find boats for hire located here. The City Dock is off Spa Creek, which forms one boundary of Annapolis, College Creek and the Severn River forming the other sides. From this point there is a nice view of the city, dominated by the State House dome.

FROZEN IN . . . In 1936 a cold spell descended on the bay and froze it over so completely that it was possible to walk across the ice. These boats had fled to Spa Creek seeking shelter from the storms but the cold overtook them, freezing them tight for weeks.

ANCIENT CITY . . . Quaint is the word for Taylor Street as seen from Legum's Corner in Annapolis. The curving thoroughfare is a favorite spot for photographers and artists who try to catch some of the charm of the old city, frequently called Crabtown.

SAINT JOHN'S COLLEGE . . . On College Avenue is St. John's College, founded in 1784. It is one of the oldest colleges in the nation and one of the most unusual. Its educational program is designed around the one hundred great books. Only recently were co-eds permitted to enroll; some years ago a president who urged the admittance of the ladies had to resign. The building on the left is McDowell Hall; beyond it is Woodward Hall. The latter houses the library, which includes some books that were brought from England in 1696 to form the Colony's first public library. In front of Woodward Hall stands the famous Liberty Tree, a tulip tree said to be more than 400 years old. In Revolutionary days patriotic meetings were held beneath it and from these it gained its name.

THE NAVAL ACADEMY . . . In front of Bancroft Hall, named for George Bancroft, who inspired the naval school in 1845, the midshipmen assemble. The brigade is housed in Bancroft. This building has murals depicting famous naval battles and, in Memorial Hall, has relics including the flag that Perry's ship flew during the battle of Lake Erie. It was there the famous commander uttered the words, "Don't give up the ship." The Academy grounds stretch along the Severn River and a beautiful view of the buildings may be had from the shore opposite, as is shown in the lower photograph.

THE GOD OF 2.5 . . . This bronze replica of the U.S.S. Delaware's figurehead is Tecumseh, the god of 2.5, the Academy's passing grade. Perfect is 4.0. Pennies are tossed at him to gain his help in getting better grades or other boons such as a lovely drag (girl) for one of the hops (dances).

NAVAL ACADEMY CHAPEL . . . Here the midshipmen attend non-denominational services every Sunday. The dome towers more than two hundred feet. In a crypt beneath the Chapel are contained the sarcophagus of John Paul Jones and many historic relics. The stained glass windows commemorate Naval heroes.

WHITEHALL . . . Built in 1765, this beautiful Anne Arundel County home was erected by slaves and indentured servants. In 1930 it was selected by the Baltimore Chapter of the American Institute of Architects as the most typical example of early Colonial architecture in the state. It was the home of Governor Horatio Sharpe, one of the last of the provincial governors, and is an almost perfect example of the Colonial five part construction. The spacious grounds overlook the Chesapeake Bay.

FRIENDSHIP INTERNATIONAL AIRPORT . . . Situated in nearby Anne Arundel County is Baltimore's Friendship International Airport, one of the most modern and most beautiful in the nation. With an eye to the future, its runways are long enough to accommodate, with room to spare, the largest ships in use today—and those which are likely to be built in the future. Travelers arriving at the airport are whisked to Baltimore over a new high speed expressway leading to the center of the city. The trip takes only 20 minutes.

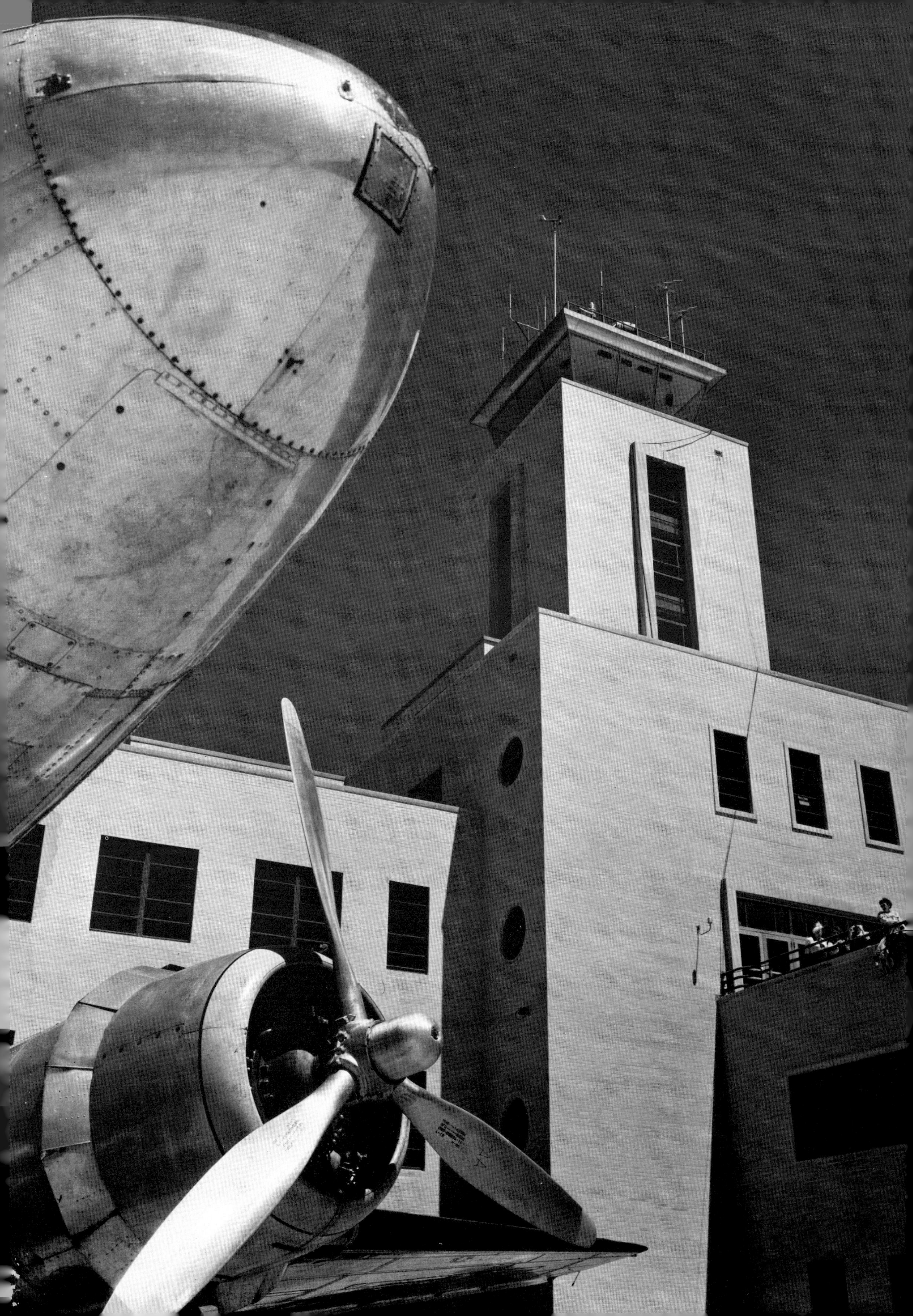

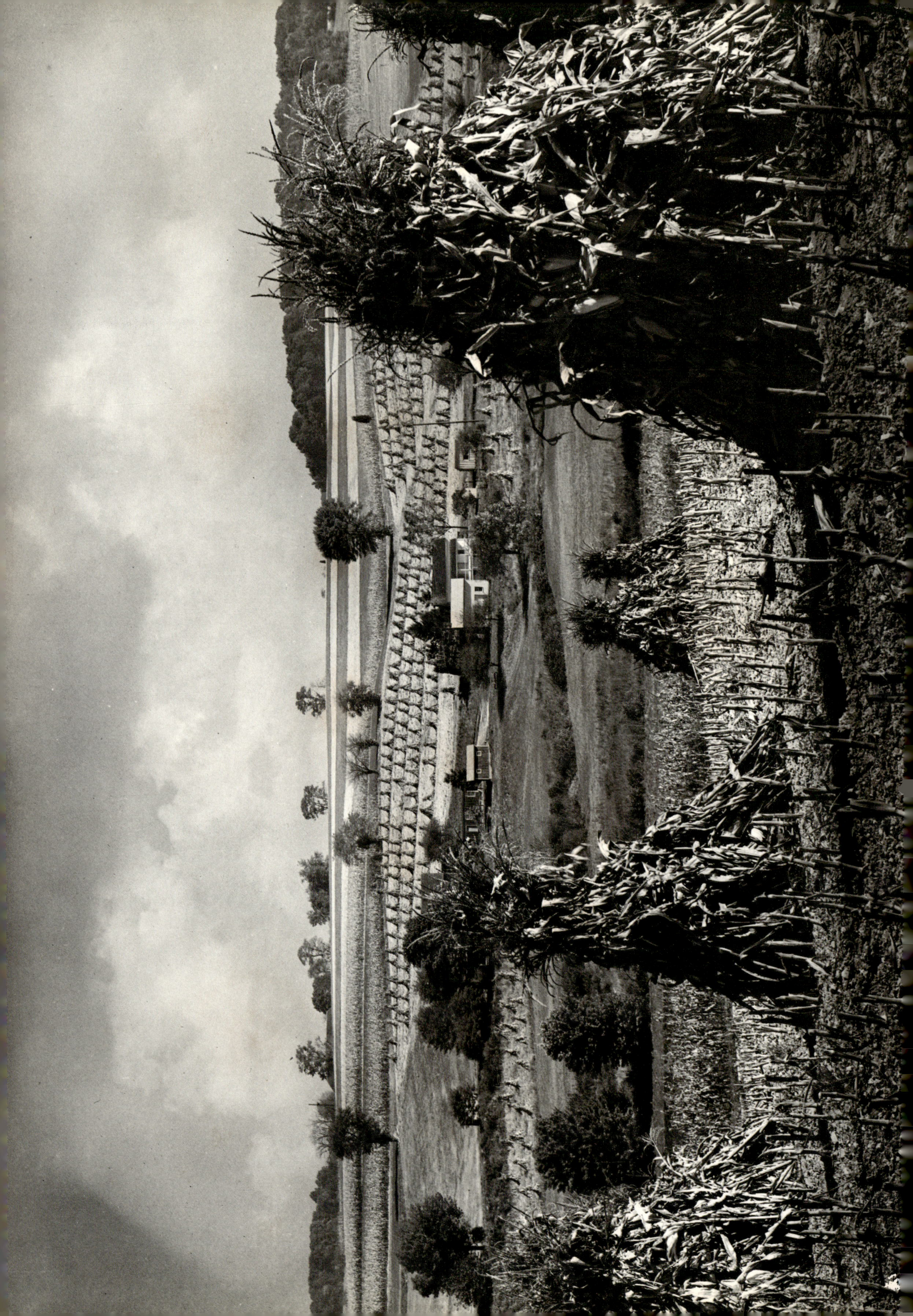

INDIAN CORN . . . Some of the early German influence is still evident in Carroll County. Roaming over the gently rolling hills, one can always see here and there a fine brick house with massive barns nearby and the whole enclosed by lacelike fences; fences also rim the cultivated fields. In contrast, the early English settlers were "croppers," setting out tobacco and light crops; only the Germans went in for the heavier farming.

GREAT FALLS OF THE POTOMAC . . . At Great Falls Park in Montgomery County there is an excellent view of the cataracts of the Potomac River. Here also are remnants of several of George Washington's ventures: a part of his iron foundry and the walls of his mill. The park also includes recreational facilities and areas, with boating available on a flooded section of the old Chesapeake and Ohio Canal.

CHAPEL, COLLEGE PARK

CHAPEL, COLLEGE PARK . . . In Prince Georges County, just eight miles from Washington, is College Park, the home of the University of Maryland. On the campus there stands this $1,000,000 edifice, serving the religious needs of the thousands of students who live in the university dormitories and nearby private residences. Altars are so designed that any type of service can be held, and there is a special inner chapel for Roman Catholic students.

HARD BARGAIN . . . This is one of the so-called "telescope houses," built in sections that are progressively smaller. The house was built before 1776. According to an old legend, two brothers sought the hand of the same girl. At the wedding, the winning brother offered to build the loser a fine house if he would kiss the bride. The loser did, and Hard Bargain was built for him. The house stands in Charles County, where it overlooks the Wicomico River.

Thomas Viaduct and the Royal Blue

BUILT TO LAST . . . The Thomas Viaduct over the Patapsco River between Relay and Elk Ridge Landing is the oldest stone arch railroad bridge in the world. Built in 1835 to take the "grasshopper" engines of those days, it is still in service; trains of all sizes and weights have stood still upon it, crawled over it and flashed across it, but never a stone has fallen, never an arch has quaked. The picture shows the Baltimore and Ohio streamliner Royal Blue crossing it. Irish contractor John McCartney, when the span was completed, erected a monument at his own expense putting his own name on it in two places in addition to the names of the B & O directors and officers, and other officials connected with its building. The bridge cost $142,236.51 in 1835. Today stone masons no longer are available to do this kind of work, but even if they could be found, one arch would cost many times that.

CONOCOCHEAGUE BRIDGE . . . At Williamsport in Washington County, at the confluence of the Potomac River and Conococheague Creek, stands this bridge. This place was the junction of many important Indian trails and a great fording spot for the wagon trains on their way to the west. The town of Williamsport was laid out in 1786 by a General Williams and a petition was sent to Congress to have it named the "Federal City," the capital of the nation. Washington inspected it in 1790. The petition was denied because large vessels could not reach the place, being blocked by the falls of the Potomac farther downstream. Evidences of Indian occupation of this spot are numerous and Indian artifacts are constantly being turned up. Washington County, which lies in the western part of the state, bordering the Pennsylvania line, was the first Washington County in the United States.

DOUGHOREGAN MANOR . . . In Howard County stands this fine home, now occupied by the seventh generation of the descendants of Charles Carroll of Carrollton, the last of the signers of the Declaration of Independence to survive. The house is three hundred feet long and the central section dates back to 1727. In one ell is a Roman Catholic Chapel used in the days when services were conducted privately. Carroll was a brilliant man and at the time of his death in 1832 was known as the richest man in America.

ELLICOTT CITY . . . Situated along the banks of the Patapsco River is the city founded by the three sons of Andrew Ellicott, who set up a flour mill there in 1774. When the Cumberland Road to the west was built and followed by the railroad, the town grew rapidly. The houses are built of native granite and appear to be built right into the rocky hillside.

WHEAT FOR THE MILLS . . . On the upland farms the swaying fields of wheat and other grains are a common sight. Wheat was one of the early crops of importance and at one time taxes were collected in bushels of wheat. While the pictures were taken in Charles County (top) and Baltimore County (lower) they are typical of scenes enacted in many sections of the state.

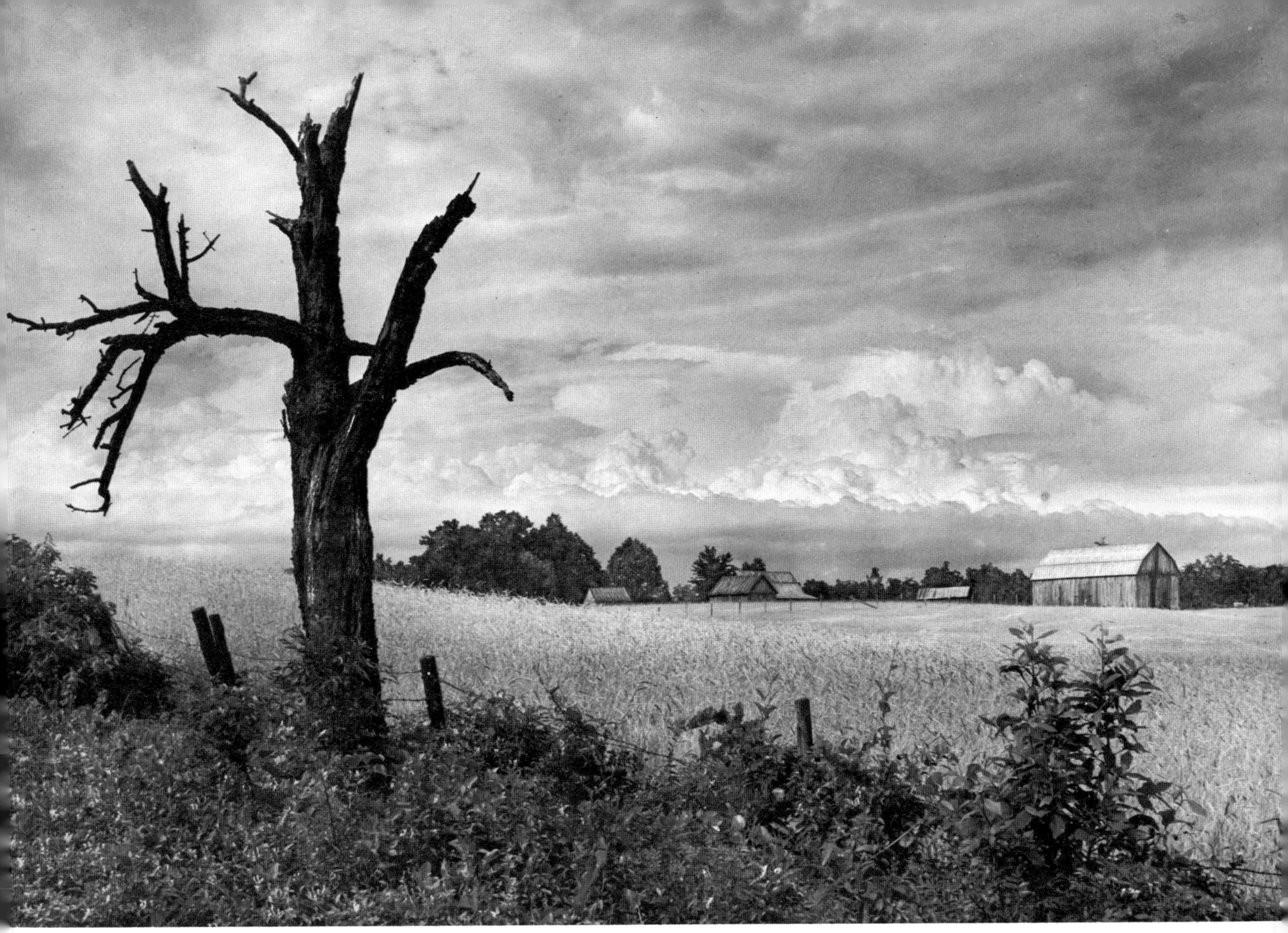

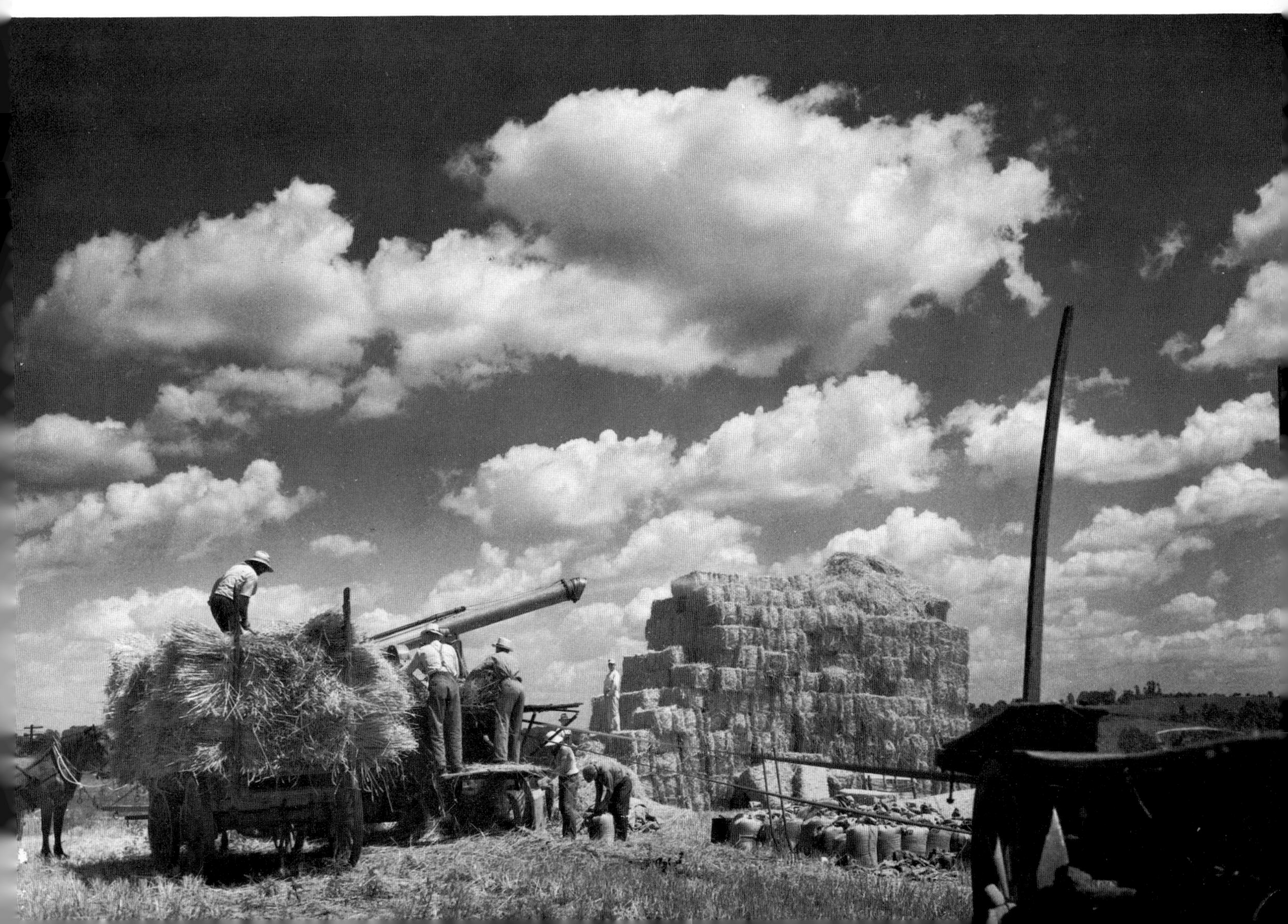

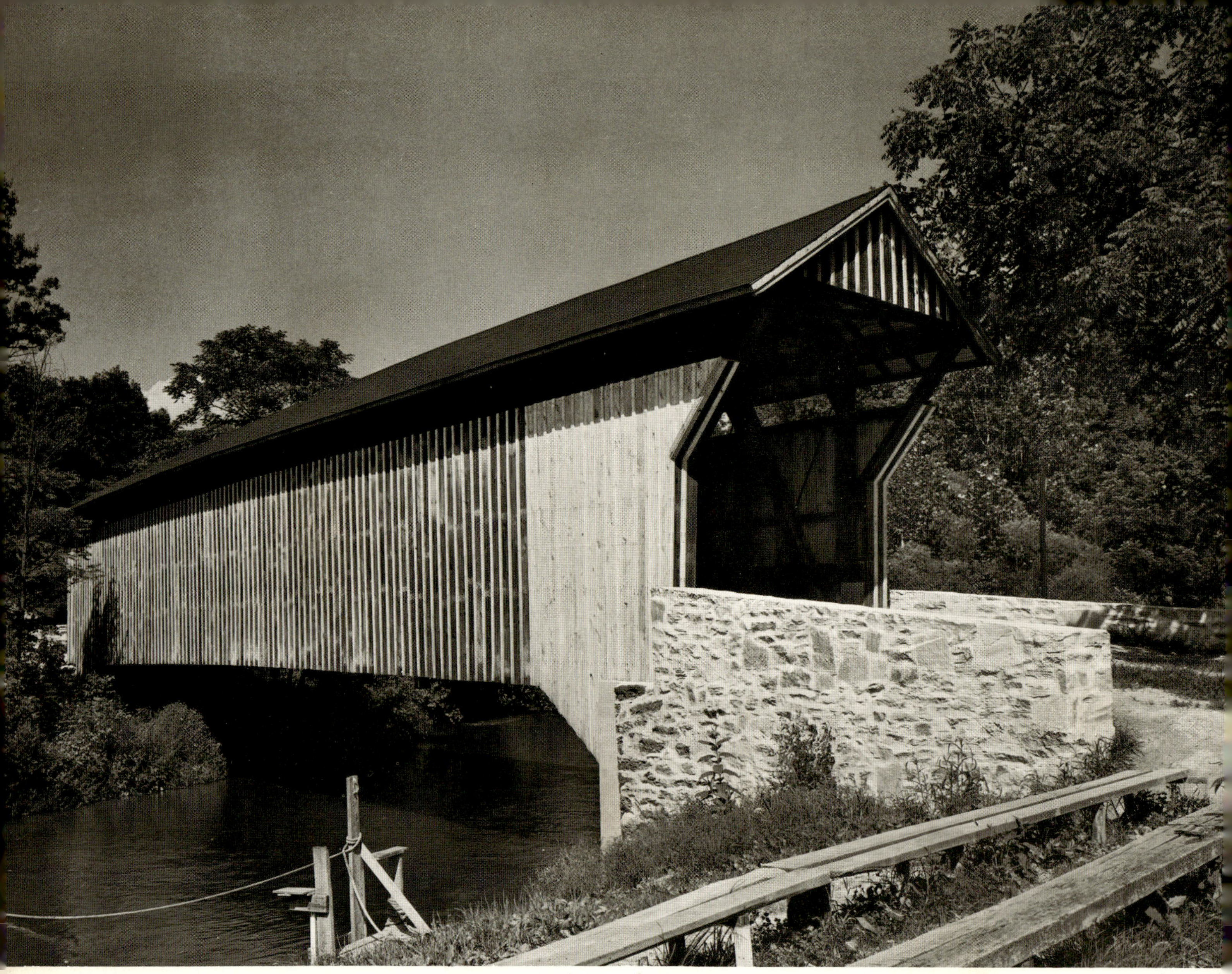

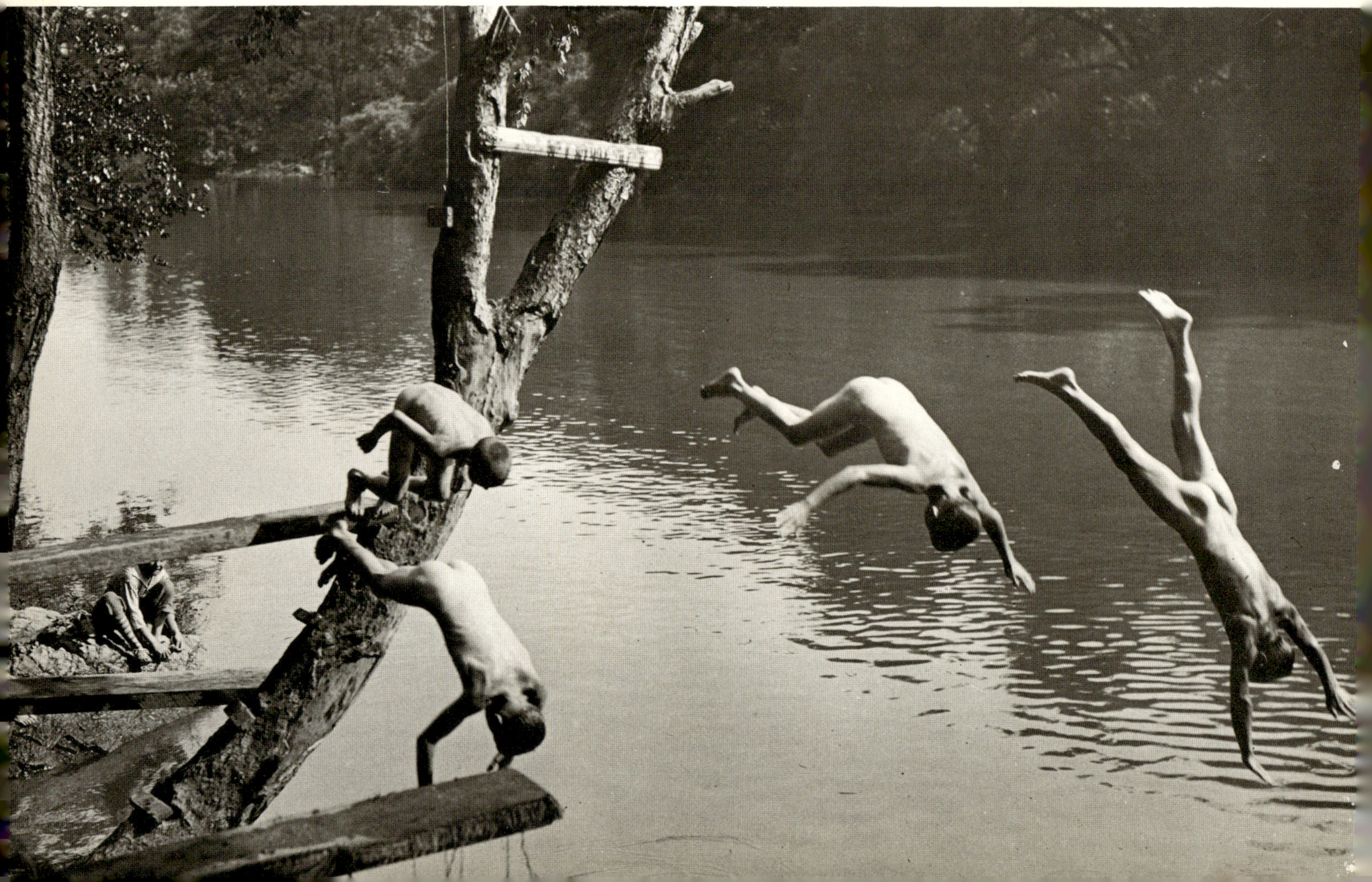

COVERED BRIDGES . . . There are eleven covered bridges still in use in Maryland, but only four counties have any at all. This bridge is on the Bunker Hill Road below Pretty Boy Dam. It was built in 1880 and was recently restored to its original condition. The bridges were covered to prevent all ravages of weather on the oak beams and not just to keep off the snow.

THE OLD SWIMMING HOLE . . . Country youngsters today have just as much fun as their Colonial ancestors and the old swimming holes are as attractive as ever. These youngsters were taking their swim in the Patapsco River near Avalon in the Patapsco State Park.

AMOS MILL . . . In Harford County near Norrisville is this old grist mill, still operating in the same old way after 200 years. Farmers bring their grain to be ground and the miller takes his pay or share for grinding it. Power for the millstone is furnished by the waters of Deer Creek which fall over the water wheel on the side of the mill. This type of wheel is called an overshot wheel in contrast to the usual type, the undershot, where the water pushes the wheel from the bottom. The corn or other grain is ground by the millstones, or burrs, a slow grinding process, quite unlike the modern turbine powered mill. This gives the meal or flour a sweeter taste.

COOK'S TOUR . . . Old fashioned apple butter is made in great copper kettles, outdoors, and its making usually brings together a party of friends and neighbors. This scene took place in Harford County.

MAKING PUDDIN' . . . This also is a time when families get together and share the work—and the great country meals—of ham, chicken, sauerkraut, potatoes, beans, tomatoes, corn, and three kinds of pie.

THE GOOD EARTH . . . The soil of Maryland is fertile and the different parts of the state are suited to the raising of a large variety of crops. Southern Maryland and the bay shores produce crops requiring light, loamy soils while in the middle counties the soils are heavier. Here a farmer turns the rich, brown earth, following the newer practice of contour plowing, about which his ancestors knew nothing.

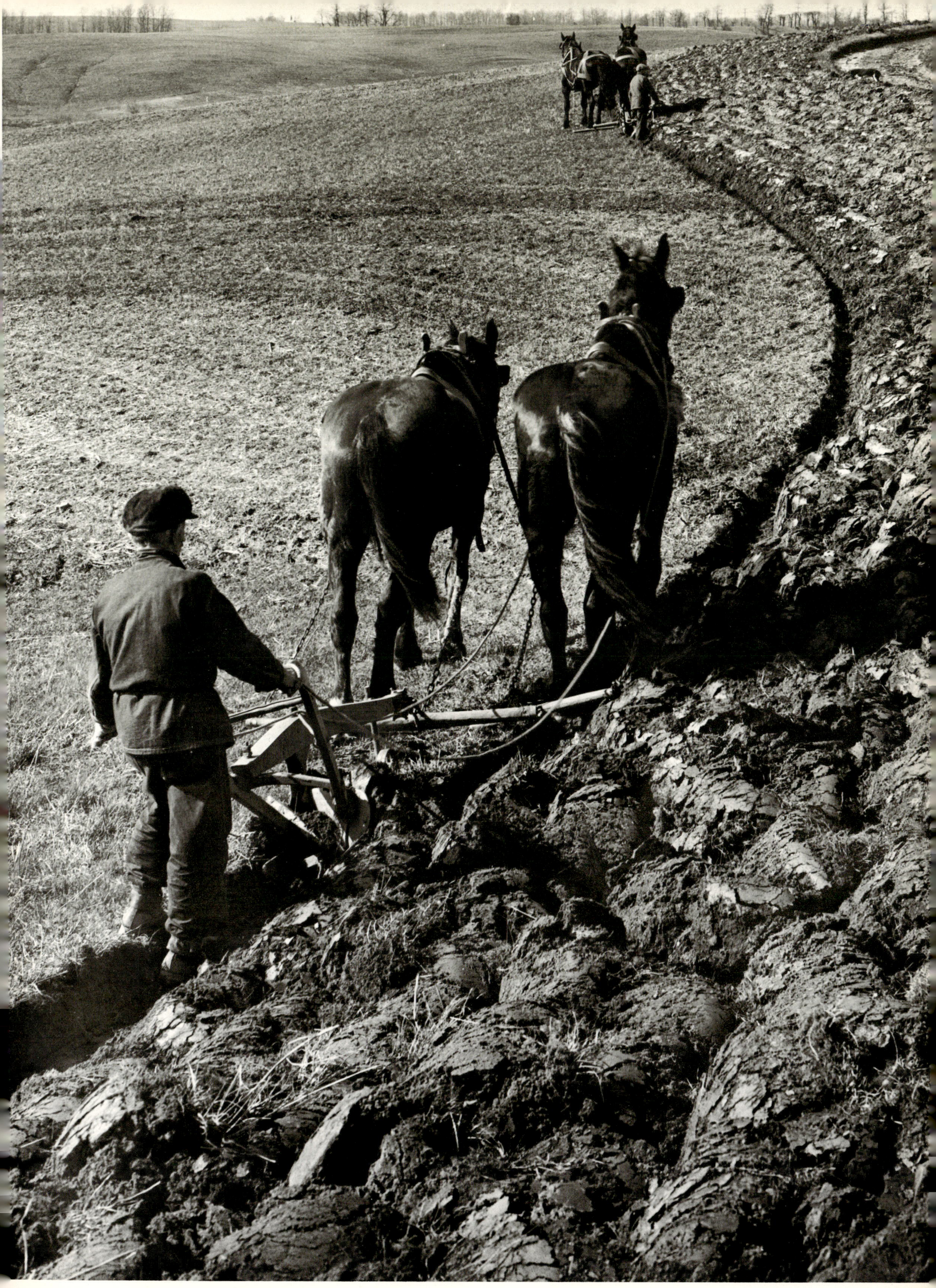

POUND NETTERS . . . On the Susquehanna flats where the river enters the bay in Harford and Cecil Counties, the fishermen set out their nets during the herring run, as shown here. The nets, tied to stakes shoved into the mud, are shaped into a funnel which leads the fish to the "trap." The Susquehanna flats make up a 50-square-mile area famous for its canvasback duck hunting. The ducks feed upon the acres and acres of wild celery, which flavors them.

FISHING CREEK . . . In the Catoctin Mountains in Frederick County is this well stocked trout stream which runs within a few miles of Shangri La, President Franklin Roosevelt's vacation hideout during the war.

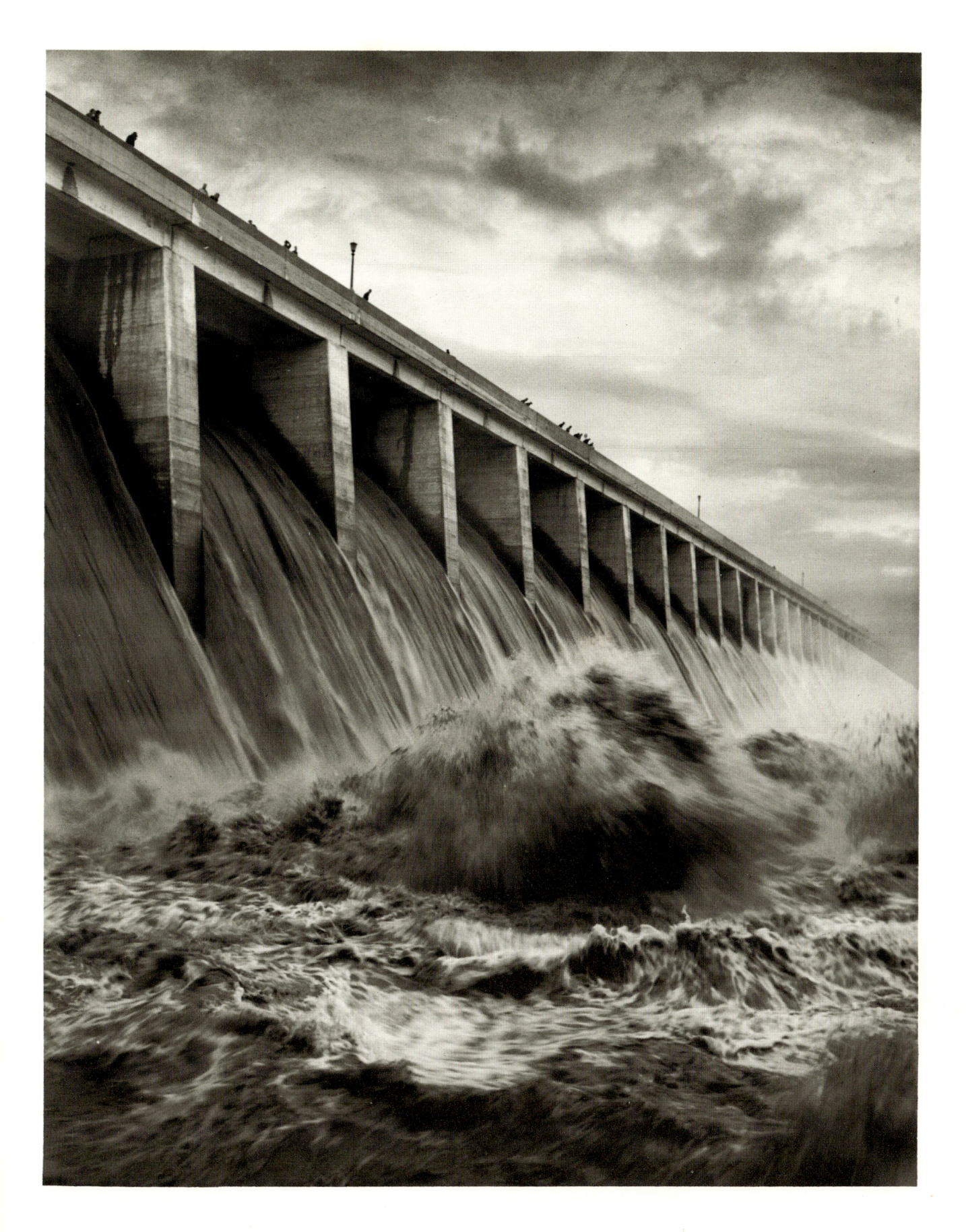

AND THE FLOODS CAME . . . The 1936 flood was the greatest ever reported on the Susquehanna; over 5,700,000 gallons a second! Indeed it was the greatest known for any non-navigable river. The giant Conowingo hydro-electric power plant opened its fifty large gates and the three regulating gates, allowing 20,500 cubic feet of water per second to pass.

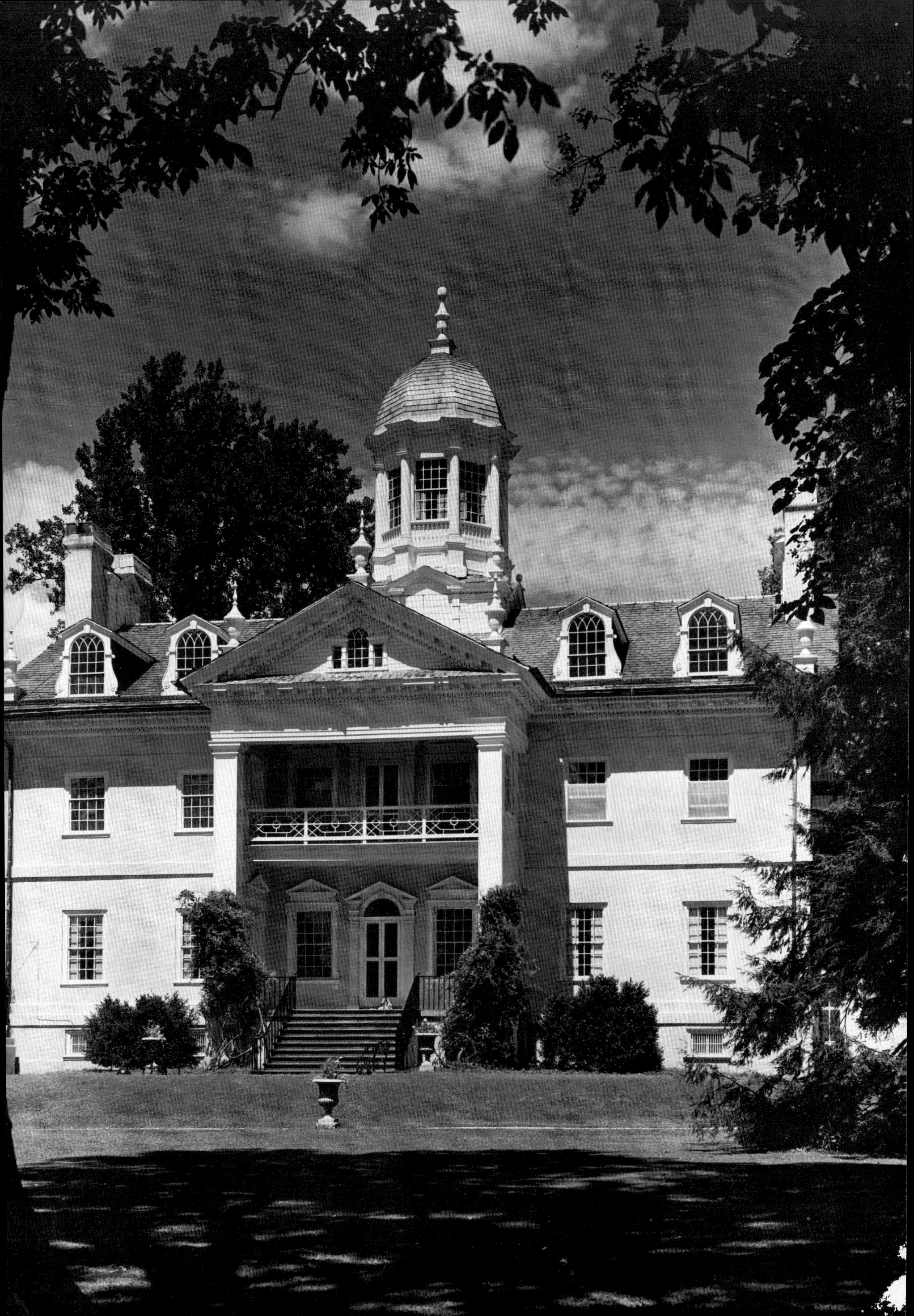

HAMPTON HOUSE . . . Built by Charles Ridgely, it is one of the largest of the early houses in Maryland and one of the few with stucco as an outside wall finish. The building was started in 1783 and Charles Ridgely died in 1790, just six months after the house had been completed. It has extensive gardens, and the ruins of an Orangery can be seen on the grounds. It was occupied by the Ridgelys for 162 years; then it was purchased by the Avalon Trust founded by Mrs. Ailsa Mellon Bruce, and presented to the Federal Government. Hampton is administered by the National Park Service, and the Society for the Preservation of Maryland Antiquities acts as custodian. All money for upkeep and improvement comes from the small admission fee, the rental of a tea room in part of the house, and gifts to the society by interested individuals.

OVER THE BARS . . . The Maryland Hunt Cup race in the Worthington Valley is considered to be the equivalent of the British Grand National. The course has a fine natural layout that permits the visitor to have an ideal view of the four-mile point-to-point race with its many jumps and hazards. The first Maryland Hunt Cup was run in 1894, which makes this the oldest point-to-point race in America. The early Colonial families were much interested in horses, not only from the standpoint of using them for work, but for racing and fox hunting, which they had been accustomed to enjoy in England. The valley is a natural amphitheater and can hold thirty thousand spectators. The first race of the season in Maryland is that of My Lady's Manor. This is followed by the Grand National and then the Maryland Hunt Cup.

SUNRISE IN THE VALLEY ... Just to the north of Baltimore, in Baltimore County, are four famous valleys, Greenspring, Worthington, Dulany and Long Green. In them are found many great estates and fine homes, most of the latter built comparatively recently although there are a goodly number of Colonial dwellings. This is one of the most beautiful areas in the state accessible to a large city.

HUNTING THE FOX . . . Maryland has nine large hunt clubs aside from other smaller groups, and fox hunting is a well followed sport in the state. Both the red and grey foxes are plentiful so it is not necessary to drag the anise seed bag over a course before the start of a hunt. A quaint custom carried over the Atlantic by the early English was that of blessing the hounds on Thanksgiving Day. This ceremony takes place at Saint John's Church in the Worthington Valley. The first recorded fox hunt took place in Queen Annes County in 1650.

CHESTNUT RIDGE . . . A typical agricultural scene in Baltimore County, with the chestnut rail fences dividing the fertile farmland. The average Maryland farm covers 102 acres, and its average production is valued at over $5000. There is competition in farming, as in other businesses, and the modern farmer must keep pace with new methods if he is to succeed.

107

"BLOOM TOWN," MARYLAND . . . At Lilypons, in Frederick County, can be found the world's largest center for goldfish and exotic plants. Named for the famous opera star, who has her Christmas cards postmarked there every year, and visits the spot when she can, it serves the Three Springs Fisheries, which annually ship over 90,000,000 fish to many countries. A hundred varieties of lilies grow in the 700 rearing ponds, which also contain the fish.

90,000,000 FISH . . . Puss could lead a fattening life if permitted to eat the goldfish at the fisheries.

TAYLORSVILLE FARM . . . Typical of Maryland's beautiful rural settings is this farm in Carroll County.

MELLOWED IN WOOD . . . This pump is made from sections of hollow logs. They are hooked together in a single length, fifty feet long, and you haven't tasted cool, cool water until you have drunk from it.

OIL FOR WORMS . . . Carroll County leads the world in the production of wormseed oil; in fact it has a world monopoly. The oil is distilled from the plants.

109

RANSOMED TOWN . . . During the Civil War the Confederate army occupied Frederick and General Early demanded that $200,000 be raised or the town would be sacked. The money was forthcoming and afterward the banks floated a loan to repay the townspeople for their contributions. Every year a part of the tax money was set aside for this bond issue and in September, 1951, the final payment was made, eighty-eight years after the demand! The Barbara Fritchie House, from the window of which Barbara Fritchie was supposed to have defied Stonewall Jackson and his army with her famous "Shoot if you must this old, gray head," is situated in Frederick. Whether the incident actually occurred as related in Whittier's poem there is some reason to doubt.

FIRST WASHINGTON MONUMENT . . . While the City of Baltimore was raising the funds to build the huge monument on Charles Street, Boonsboro was thinking about one. The monument in Baltimore was started in 1809 and finished in 1829. On July 4th, 1827, the citizens of Boonsboro completed this monument in one day and thus became the possessors of the first monument in the United States to be completed in honor of George Washington. The structure fell to pieces about the time of the Civil War but it was restored in 1936. It is to be found in Washington Monument State Park above Zittlestown, which was named after a family that settled there. The area was much involved in the Civil War campaigns and the spot used as a Union signal tower.

WASHINGTON MONUMENT, BOONSBORO

MIDDLETOWN VALLEY . . . One of the loveliest and most fertile valleys in the state as seen from Gambrill State Park at 1600 feet altitude. Here the valley spreads southward toward the Potomac and westward toward South Mountain. Throughout this section the German influence is very evident, with beautiful homes, barns, and orderly fields.

NO MORTAR . . . The Chesapeake and Ohio Canal aqueduct is a marvel of stone masonry, for no mortar was used in its construction; instead the coursed rubble masonry is pinned together with square malleable iron pins. It crosses the Monocacy River at its confluence with the Potomac. The structure was begun in 1824 and completed in 1827 and has withstood devastating floods for over a century.

TRI-STATE VIEW . . . Where Maryland is narrowest three states can be seen as shown in this picture. The camera was at Lovers Leap in West Virginia, with the Potomac river beneath. Bordering the river is the C and O Canal, then comes a railroad, and beyond that lie the National pike and the rolling hills of Pennsylvania. Slightly west of Hancock the state is only four miles wide, a good spot to be in if one wants to skip the sheriff.

BLOODIEST BATTLE . . . At Antietam in Washington County was fought the bloodiest one-day battle of the Civil War. The battle took place on September 17, 1862. Federal losses were 12,410 and Confederate losses 10,700 in killed or wounded. One Federal corps marched into a pocket of ten Confederate brigades and lost 2000 men in twenty minutes. Northerners call it the Battle of Antietam, Southerners the Battle of Sharpsburg. The Confederates withdrew.

CATOCTIN FURNACE . . . This Frederick County settlement got its start from an iron furnace which opened in 1774, and it has changed but little since. All the log cabins and stone buildings are spotlessly whitewashed. The Catoctin Furnace supplied cannon balls used in the siege of Yorktown.

FORT FREDERICK . . . This fort, which is in Washington County, was built during the French and Indian War. It has walls seventeen feet high, is typical of fortifications of the middle 1700's, and is regarded as an especially fine relic of that era. It was garrisoned again during the Revolution—when a few Redcoats were captured there—and during the Civil War.

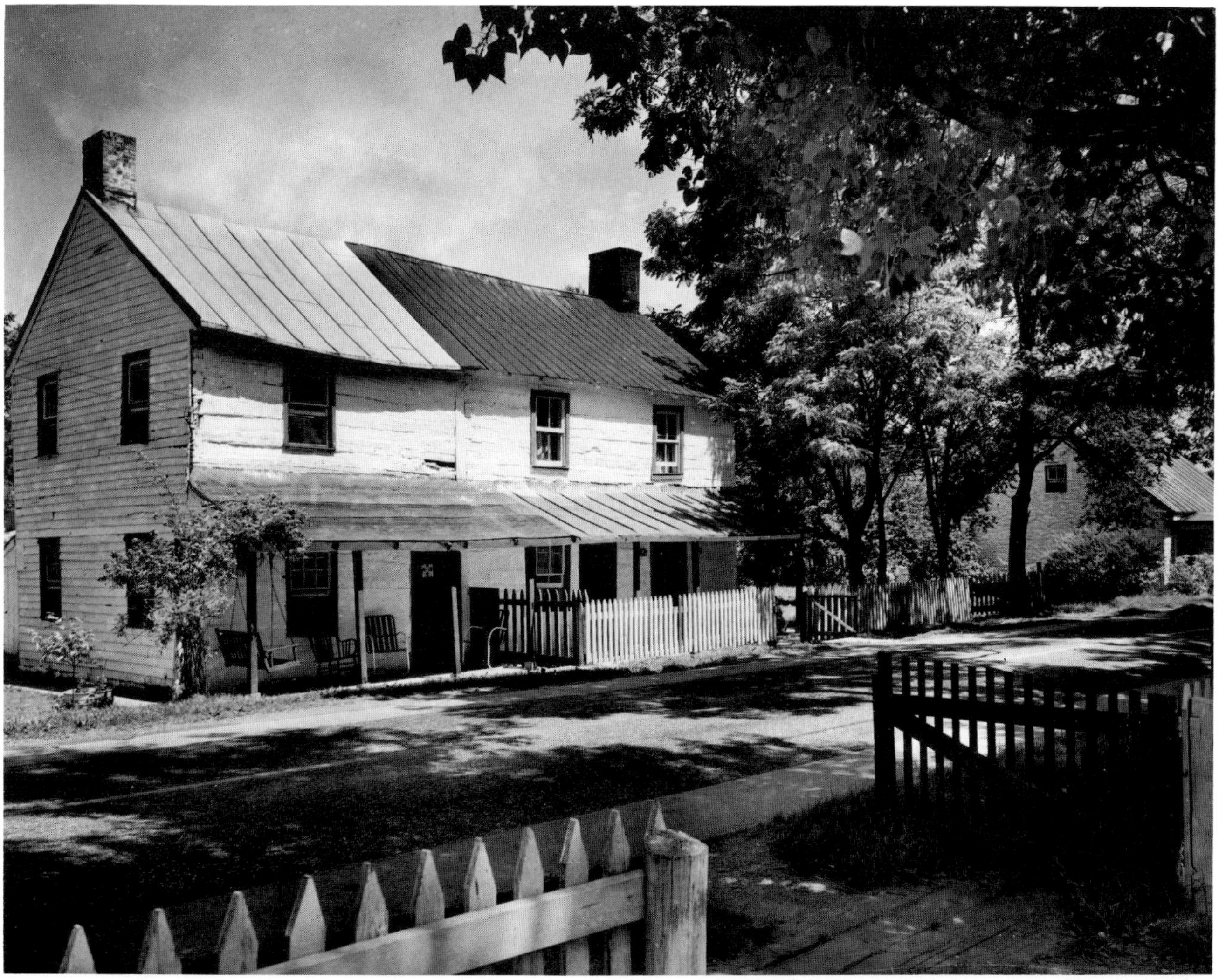

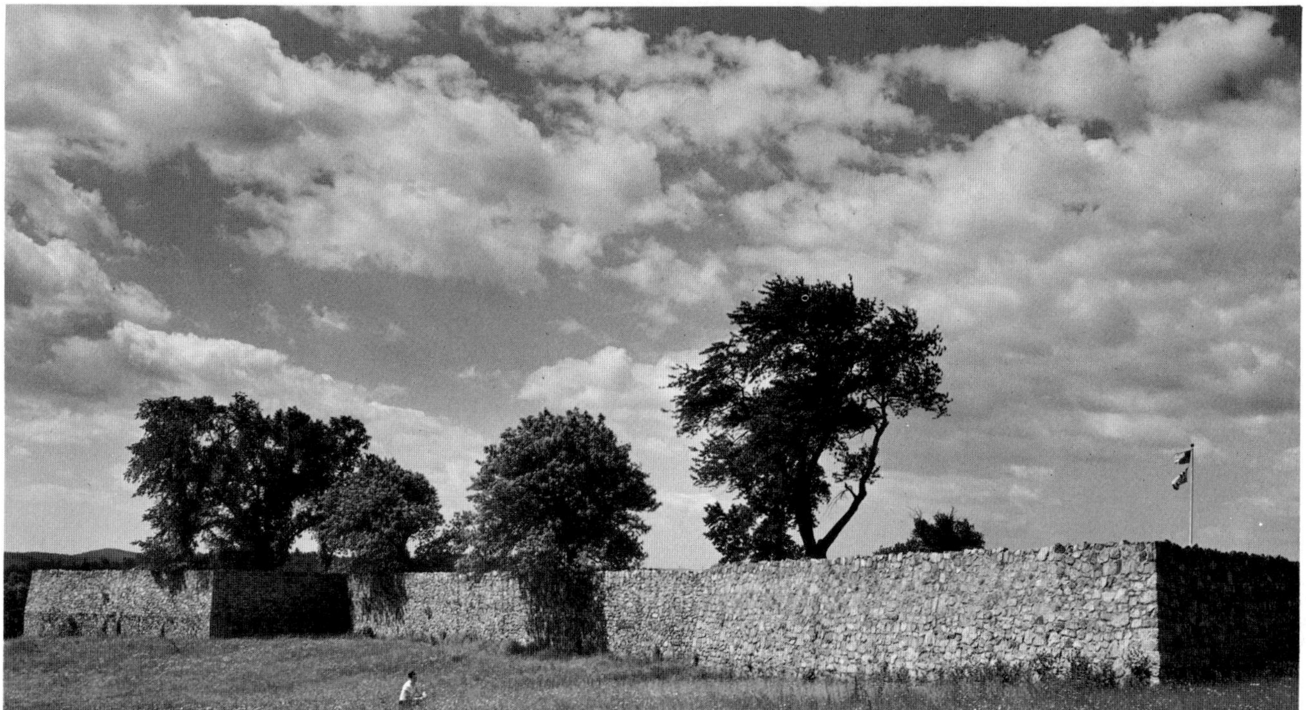

ANTIETAM FURNACE BRIDGE

ANTIETAM FURNACE BRIDGE . . . Built in 1827, this stone arched bridge took its name from the Antietam Iron Works, the ruins of which are nearby. Cannon balls and shells were cast at the iron works for the Revolutionary War and afterward the works turned to making peaceful items such as Dutch ovens, household and farm articles. When James Rumsey was experimenting with his first steam boat in 1785, some of the parts were made here. His boat is believed to have been the first ever to travel upstream under its own power. Out of nineteen stone arched bridges built across Antietam Creek more than a century ago, seventeen are still in use today.

ABOVE THE FRUITED PLAIN . . . This view was made on Tonoloway Mountain, west of Hancock in Washington County. Here is the center of Maryland's apple production; it is a part of the famous Appalachian apple belt, one of the finest apple and peach growing regions in the east. Washington County has more than three hundred thousand apple trees and in the peak year more than three million bushels were grown. Washington County also ranks high in the growing of grains, and the fattening of cattle for market is an important part of farming. The raspberries which are picked from the mountain bushes find a ready market.

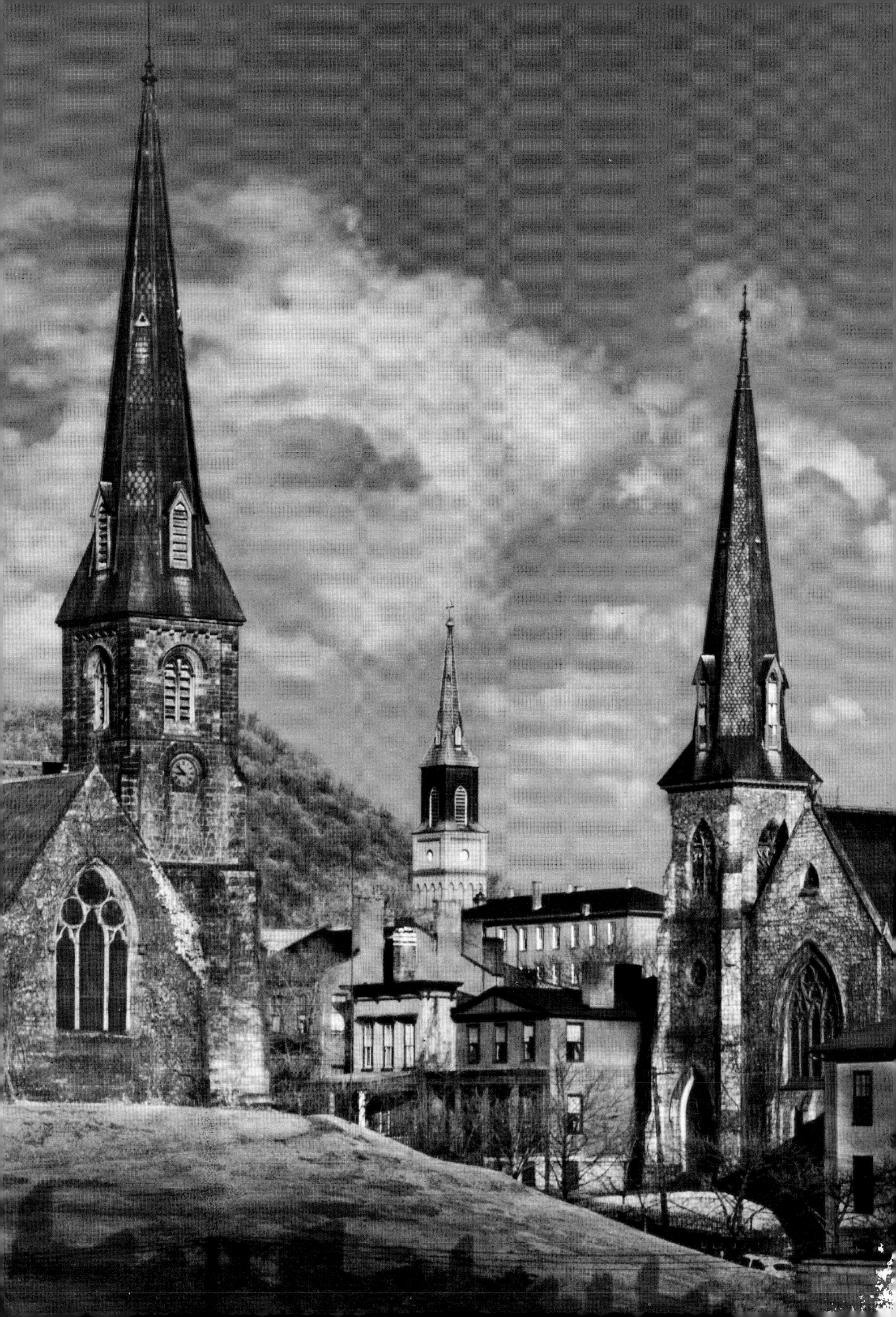

CUMBERLAND . . . Now Maryland's second city, Cumberland has grown to that size from a beginning as a mere trading post in 1750. In 1754 George Washington launched the building there of a fort the remnants of which—a series of tunnels running down to Wills Creek—lie partly under Emmanuel Protestant Episcopal Church, the edifice nearest the camera in this photograph. The church in the center is that of SS. Peter and Paul, Roman Catholic, and that on the right is the First Presbyterian.

MODERN KNIGHTS . . . The Age of Chivalry lives on in Maryland through frequent Tournaments in which riders tilt their lances at little rings. Three charges are made down the course in quest of nine circlets that decrease in diameter from an initial inch and a quarter. The winner crowns a Queen of Love and Beauty. This scene was at Clear Spring, Washington County.

CROWN STONE . . . Marking the Mason and Dixon line between Maryland and Pennsylvania are stones set every mile along the way. Every fifth stone is a crown stone, bearing the coat of arms of the Calverts on one side and that of William Penn on the other. The mile stones have M and P incised on their Maryland and Pennsylvania sides.

UPSPOUTS . . . At Keedysville, Boonsboro, Williamsport, New Market and Libertytown the rainspouts, instead of going down, go straight out from the roofs. Woe betide the unwary traveler who should happen to park under one of these and leave his car windows open, for a sudden shower from the mountains could fill the car with water.

UNDOUBTEDLY . . . This amusing combination of signs in Cambridge unwittingly states a truth.

SAINT MARK'S EPISCOPAL CHURCH . . . This is one of the most attractive churches in Western Maryland. It is situated at Breathedsville, Washington County, and serves Antietam Parish. So small, dainty and quaint is its interior that it suggests a scene "Behind the Looking Glass." There are but twenty-one pews—six of which are occupied by a choir of thirty-two members. The first wedding performed in St. Mark's was that of Jeremiah and Melinda, slaves, on Christmas Day in 1849, the year in which the church was built.

SAINT MARK'S EPISCOPAL CHURCH, BREATHEDSVILLE

FISHING HOLE . . . At lock 71 of the old Chesapeake and Ohio Canal, at Oldtown, is the Battie Mixon fishing hole. The canal has been flooded for a distance of four and a half miles and has been well stocked with fish. During the canal's heyday Oldtown thrived, but with the closing of the canal it slipped away. Today it is just what its name implies and only a few homes remain, the most famous of which is the Cresap house, which was built by the son of the first white settler in the region, a Thomas Cresap, who arrived about 1741. The house of Michael Cresap was erected about 1765. Michael spent his entire life fighting Indians, clearing wilderness and trading. The father was called the "Maryland Monster" by the Pennsylvanians, who captured him in a border dispute, for even when shackled he threw men around with ease. They were sorry that they had captured such a strong man; he made life miserable for them, even refusing his freedom in order to get revenge on them. With his son he ran the Maryland wilderness pretty much to suit himself and everyone passing through stopped to see him for his settlement was a point on the trail to the west. He was a generous man and a tough one. Stories tell how he visited England when he was seventy years old, remarried when he was eighty, visited Nova Scotia at one hundred, and died when he was a hundred and six. He might almost be considered the eastern version of Paul Bunyan.

HIGHEST FALLS . . . In the Swallow Falls State Forest are two lovely waterfalls. Muddy Creek Falls is the highest in the state, the waters plunging seventy feet. Swallow Falls, from which the state forest gets its name, is not so spectacular in height but is none the less beautiful. In the forest, which contains over 7000 acres at an elevation of from 2200 to 2900 feet, are stands of virgin timber that are considered to be some of the finest in the east. White pine and hemlock predominate and moss covered logs from trees which fell over centuries ago are of interest. The park is the state's most westerly, located in Garrett County near Oakland.

CALLING ALL PANCAKES . . . Maple syrup time traditionally begins about Washington's Birthday. Garrett County is the state's only producer of maple products, but there the tank wagon which gathers the sap from the buckets hung on the trees is a familiar sight at syrup time. Transported to the cooking shed, the sap is boiled and reduced to syrup and sugar. The buckets used on the trees are called keelers and the sap collected is called maple water. About 18,000 gallons are produced in a season. The picture was made near Grantsville, the highest town in the state, while the snow was still on the ground.

FROM UNDERGROUND . . . Mining and quarrying are both important Maryland industries; large deposits of soft coal occur, though confined to the western counties. The quarry shown produces a green marble; it is situated on the state line at Cardiff, Harford County. This is the only source of such stone in the nation. The cut goes down 321 feet.

THE POTOMAC . . . This is how the famous river looks at Doe Gully in Allegany County, a beautiful sight to behold near the close of day. Farther downstream it passes through industrial towns, and then after dropping over the Great Falls near Washington it becomes a navigable river and flows on into the Chesapeake Bay. The Potomac is a Maryland river, for where it divides Maryland from Virginia the state line is at the low tide mark on the Virginia shore. This sometimes leads to amusing situations and sometimes to tragic ones— game wardens have shot and killed Virginia poachers in the river. Some Virginians, taking advantage of the fact that Maryland is a "wet" state, get a Maryland liquor license and run a pier out from the Virginia shore, putting their establishment on the end. Legally they are doing business in Maryland although the walkway begins in Virginia. The boundary is very old and has been approved by the Supreme Court. The Potomac flows in an easterly direction and cuts across the entire Appalachian mountain chain, having cut its own valley through the ages. Its end is at Point Lookout, where it enters the Chesapeake bay.

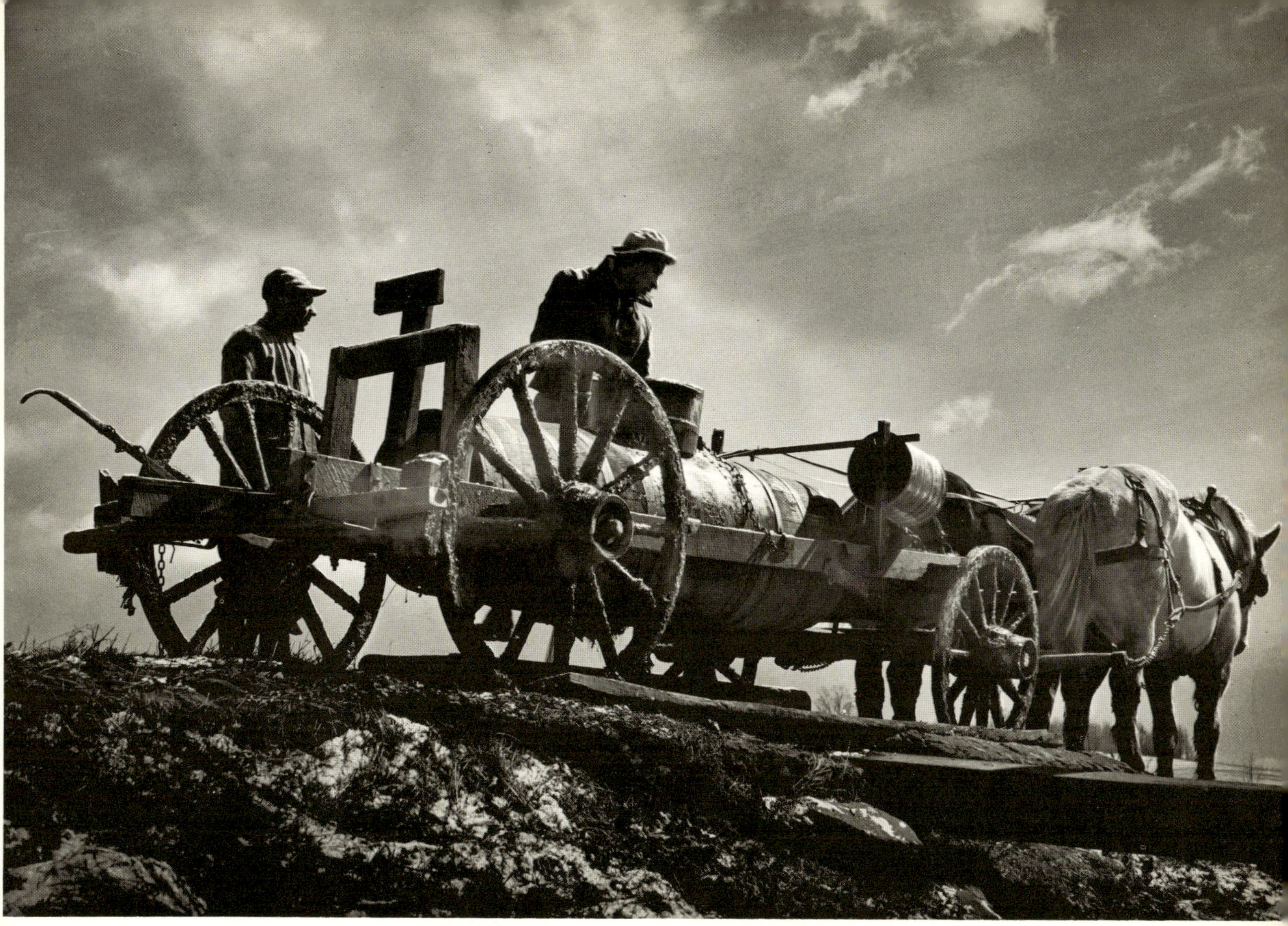

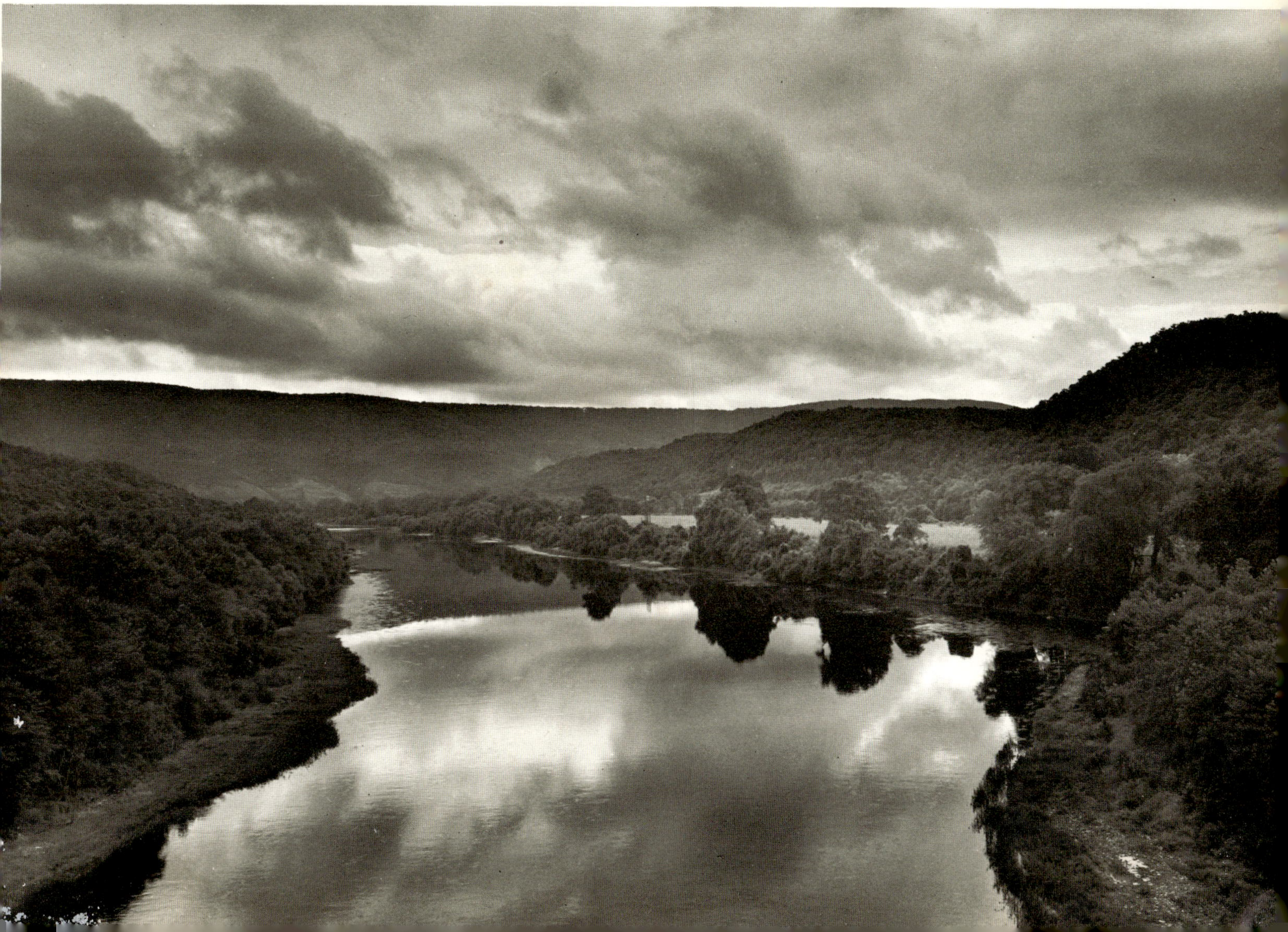

QUIET AND PEACE . . . The sun sets across the great, fertile Middletown Valley; this view is from Braddock Heights toward South Mountain, the dividing line between Frederick and Washington Counties.

# ACKNOWLEDGEMENTS

I would like to express my thanks to my wife, Nancy, for her assistance in many, many ways during the preparation of this book. To Stanley L. Cahn I owe thanks for getting the whole project under way; feeling strongly that there should be a pictorial book on Maryland, he has worked tirelessly to bring about publication of my photographs.

My appreciation also goes to J. Albert Caldwell, of Universal Lithographers, who personally supervised the printing and who was not satisfied with anything short of perfection. George M. Rowan and Mark Mooney, Jr., of Camera Magazine, did the layouts and prepared the book for publication. Editorial work on the text was done by Hervey Brackbill.

Thanks go likewise to the Baltimore Sunpapers for their permission to use the photographs that had appeared in the Sunday Sun Magazine, to Harold A. Williams for many worthwhile suggestions that have been adopted, and, finally to the countless individuals who have aided me in the field, interrupting their work or posing so that I might record a scene.

A. A. B.

---

Format and jacket design by Robert W. Lapham, of Baltimore.
Lithographed by the Unitone Process by Universal Lithographers of Baltimore.
Type set by Modern Linotypers, Inc., of Baltimore.
Lithographed on 100 pound Dullcoat Enamel manufactured by S. D. Warren Co.
Special inks by C. O. Monk of Maryland, Inc.
Binding by Moore and Co., of Baltimore.

INSOMNIA

# INDEX

Alleghany County, Potomac River-125
Anderton, Talbot County-16
Annapolis,
  City Dock, Spa Creek-82-83
  Governor's Mansion-81
  Hammond-Harwood House-3
  State House-2-80
  St. John's College-84
  Taylor Street-84
  Naval Academy,
    Bancroft Hall-85
    Chapel-87
    Severn River-85
    Tecumseh-86
Anne Arundel County,
  Friendship International Airport-89
  Tobacco-76
  Whitehall-88
Antietam, Washington County-114
Antietam Furnace Bridge-116
Amish, Newmarket, St. Mary's County-77
Apple Production, Washington County-117
Assateague Island, Surf Casting-9
Assateague Island, Cattle and Ponies-9
Atlantic Shore-6
Baltimore,
  Baltimore & Ohio RR-54-94
  Cathedral-60
  City Hall-62
  Columbus Monument-65
  Druid Hill Park-71
  Federal Hill-48-49
  Fells Point-51-55
  Flag House-69
  Gilman Hall-67
  Harbor-40
  Jackson Statue-53
  Johns Hopkins Hospital-66
  Johns Hopkins University-66
  Key Monument-64
  Lee Statue-53
  Lexington Market-70
  Long Dock-45
  Mount Clare Station-54
  Mount Vernon Place-4
  Old St. Paul's Graveyard-64
  Park Avenue, First Presbyterian Church-58
  Peabody Conservatory, Washington Place,
    Walters Art Gallery-60
  Peale Museum-69
  Pimlico Race Track-70
  Poe House-54
  Pratt Library-62
  Shaarei Tfiloh Synagogue-61
  Sherwood Gardens-56
  Shot Tower-57
  Steps-46-50-51
  Street Sign-72
  Tyson Street-68
  Washington Monument-4
Baltimore County,
  Farming-107
  Hampton House-104
  Sunrise in the Valley-106
  Wheat-97
  Dulaney Valley-106
  Greenspring Valley-106
  Long Green Valley-106
  Worthington Valley-106
    Fox Hunting-107
    Maryland Hunt Cup Race-105
    St. Johns Church-107
Bancroft Hall, Naval Academy-85
Barbara Fritchie House, Frederick-110
Beaten Biscuits-23
Bethlehem Steel Co., Sparrows Point-12-52
Bloody Point Light, Kent Island-26
Boats,
  Bay Harvest-34
  Bugeye, Catherine-29
  Buy Boat-33
  The Calvert-42
  Anthony Groves, Jr.-43
  Latrobe-42
  Log Canoe, Miles River Regatta-26-28
  The Talbot-43
  Schooners, Skipjacks-27
  Thomas Clyde-29
Bodine, A. Aubrey-7-8
Bodine, Joel Goode-7-8
Boonsboro,
  "Insomnia"-127
  Washington Monument-111
Bunker Hill Road, Covered Bridges-98
Calvert County, Tobacco-76-77
Cambridge, Street Signs-120
Caroline County, White Schoolhouse-21
Carroll County,
  Indian Corn-90
  Hollow Log Pump-109
  Taylorsville Farm-109
  Worm Oil-109
Cathedral, Baltimore-60
Catoctin Furnace, Frederick County-115
Cecil County, Herring fishing-102
Chapel, College Park, University of
  Maryland-92
Charles County,
  Hard Bargain-93
  Tobacco-76
  Wheat-97
Chesapeake Bay Bridge-37
Chesapeake and Ohio Canal-112
Chestnut Ridge, Baltimore County-107
Choptank, Oyster Dredgers-30
Churches, Cumberland-118-122
City Dock, Spa Creek, Annapolis-82-83
City Hall, Baltimore-62
Clark's Conveniency, Quaker Neck-17
College Park, Chapel, University of
  Maryland-92

Columbus Monument, Baltimore-65
Conococheague Bridge, Washington County-95
Covered Bridge, Bunker Hill Road-98
Conowingo, Susquehanna River-103
Crown Stone of Mason-Dixon Line-119
Cumberland, Churches-118-122
Deer Creek, Grist Mill, Harford County-99
Diamond-Back Terrapin-23
Dorchester County, Tomatoes-13
Doughoregan Manor, Howard County-96
Druid Hill Park, Baltimore-71
Duck Decoys, Havre de Grace-14
Duck Hunters, Talbot County-14
Dulaney Valley, Baltimore County-106
Dundalk, House Pattern-59
Easton, Third Haven Meeting House-14
Ellicott City, Patapsco River-96
Farming, Baltimore County-107
  Harford County-101
Federal Hill, Baltimore-48-49
Fells Point,
  Baltimore-51
  Ornamental Iron-55
First Presbyterian Church, Park Avenue,
  Baltimore-58
Fisheries, Frederick County-108
Fishing, Frederick County-102
Fishing Hole, Oldtown-122
Fishing, Paying Off-32
Flag House, Baltimore-69
Food, Famous Dishes-23
Fort Carroll, Patapsco River-39
Fort Frederick, Washington County-115
Fort McHenry, Baltimore-38
Fox Hunting, Worthington Valley-107
Frederick, Barbara Fritchie House-110
Frederick County,
  Catoctin Furnace-115
  Fisheries-108
  Fishing-102
Friendship International Airport, Anne
  Arundel County-89
Gambrill State Park-112
Garrett County,
  Maple Syrup-125
  Water Falls-123
Gas Lights-58-68
Gilman Hall, Baltimore-67
Great Falls Park, Montgomery County-90
Greenspring Valley, Baltimore County-106
Grist Mill, Harford County, Deer Creek-99
Governor's Mansion, Annapolis-81
Hammond-Harwood House, Annapolis-3
Hampton House, Baltimore County-104
Harbor, Baltimore-40
Hard Bargain, Charles County-93
Harford County,
  Cooks Tour-100
  Deer Creek, Grist Mill-99
  Farming-101
  Herring Fishing-102
  Mining and Quarrying-124
Havre de Grace, Duck Decoys-14
Herring Fishing, Harford and Cecil
  Counties-102
Hollow Log Pump, Carroll County-109
Hoopers Island-36
Hopkins, Johns, Hospital, Baltimore-66
Hopkins, Johns, University, Baltimore-66
Howard County, Doughoregan Manor-96
Indian Corn, Carroll County-90
"Insomnia", Boonsboro-127
Jackson Statue, Baltimore-53
Jericho Farm-8
Keedysville, Rainspouts-120
Kent County, Reid Hall-22
Kent Island,
  Bloody Point Light-26
  Log Canoeing-26
  Queen Anne's County-19
Key Monument, Baltimore-64
Lee Statue, Baltimore-53
Lexington Market, Baltimore-70
Log Canoeing, Kent Island-26
Long Dock, Baltimore-45
Long Green Valley, Baltimore County-106
Madison Street, Baltimore-63
Main Street, Smith Island-35
Maple Syrup, Garrett County-125
Maryland Fried Chicken-23
Maryland Hunt Cup Race, Worthington
  Valley-105
Mason-Dixon Line Crown Stone-119
Matapeake, Schooners and Skipjacks-27
McDowell Hall, St. John's College,
  Annapolis-84-115
Middletown Valley-112
  Sunset-126
Miles River Regatta, Log Canoeing-28
Mining and Quarrying, Harford County-124
Montgomery County, Great Falls Park-90
Mount Clare Station, Baltimore-54
Mount Vernon Place, Baltimore-4
Mulberry Fields, Potomac-75
Nassawango Furnace, Worcester County-12
Naval Academy, Annapolis
  Bancroft Hall-85
  Chapel-87
  Severn River-85
  Tecumseh-86
Newmarket, St. Mary's County-73
Old Swimming Hole, Patapsco River-98
Oldtown, Fishing Hole-122
Otwell, Talbot County-17

Oyster Dredgers, Choptank-30
Oyster Dredging-31-32
Oyster Tonging-32
Oxen-77
Park Avenue, First Presbyterian Church,
  Baltimore-58
Patapsco River,
  Ellicott City-96
  Fort Carroll-39
  Old Swimming Hole-98
  Thomas Viaduct-94
Patuxent River, Railbirds-79
Paying Off, Fishing-32
Peabody Conservatory, Baltimore-60
Peale Museum, Baltimore-69
Pimlico Race Track, Baltimore-70
Pocomoke River, Worcester County-10
Pocomoke and Tangier Sound, Shell
  Shedders-34
Poe House, Baltimore-54
Point No Point, Shad-79
Port Covington, Western Maryland Railway-41
Potomac, Alleghany County-125
Potomac, Mulberry Fields, Silk Industry-75
Pratt Library, Baltimore-62
Prince George County-Tobacco-76
Quaker Neck, Clark's Conveniency-17
Queen Anne's County, Kent Island-19
Railbirds, Patuxent River-79
Rainspouts, Keedysville-120
Reid Hall, Kent Island, Washington College-22
Schooners and Skipjacks, Matapeake-27
Seafood, Somerset County-24
Severn River, Naval Academy-85
Shaarei Tfiloh Synagogue, Baltimore-61
Shad, Point No Point-79
Sherwood Gardens, Baltimore-56
Shot Tower, Baltimore-57
Smith Island, Main Street-35
Somerset County, Seafood-24
Sotterley, St. Marys County-74
Spa Creek, City Dock, Annapolis-82-83
State House, Annapolis-2-80
State House, St. Marys-78
Star Spangled Banner, Fort McHenry-38
Steps, Baltimore-46-50-51
St. Johns College, Annapolis-84
St. Marks Episcopal Church, Washington
  County-121
St. Marys County-72
  Amish, Newmarket-73
  Sotterley-74
  Tobacco-77
St. Marys, State House-78
St. Pauls Graveyard, Baltimore-64
Street Signs, Baltimore-72
Street Signs, Cambridge-120
Sparrows Point, Bethlehem Steel Co.-12-52
Sunrise in the Valley, Baltimore County-106
Sunset, Middletown Valley-127
Surf Casting, Assateague Island-9
Susquehanna River, Conowingo-103
Talbot County,
  Anderton-16
  Duck Hunters-14
  Otwell-17
  Wye House-18
  Wye Oak-20
Tangier and Pocomoke Sounds, Shell
  Shedders-34
Taylor Street, Annapolis-84
Taylorsville Farm, Carroll County-109
Tecumseh, Naval Academy, Annapolis-86
Third Haven Meeting House, Easton-14
Thomas Viaduct, Patapsco River-94
Tobacco,
  Anne Arundel County-76
  Calvert County-76-77
  Charles County-76
  Prince George County-77
  St. Marys County-77
Tomatoes, Dorchester County-13
Tonoloway Mountain, Washington County-117
Tournament, Washington County-119
Tri-State View-113
Tyson Street, Baltimore-68
University of Maryland Chapel, College Park-92
Upper Ferry, Wicomico River-10
Van Sweringen, Gerrett-8
Walters Art Gallery, Baltimore-60
Washington College, Kent County-22
Washington County,
  Antietam-114
  Apple Production-117
  Conococheague Bridge-95
  Fort Frederick-115
  St. Marks Episcopal Church-121
  Tournament-119
Washington Monument, Baltimore-4-47
Washington Monument, Boonsboro-111
Washington Place, Baltimore-60
Water Falls, Garrett County-123
Western Maryland Railway-Port Covington-41
Wheat, Baltimore and Charles Counties-97
Whitehall, Anne Arundel County-88
White Schoolhouse, Caroline County-21
Wicomico River, Upper Ferry-10
Wilson, Louise A.-7
Woodward Hall, St. John's College,
  Annapolis-84
Worcester County,
  Nassawango Furnace-12
  Pocomoke River-11
Worm Oil, Carroll County-109
Worthington Valley, Maryland Hunt Cup
  Race-105
  St. John's Church-107
Wye House, Talbot County, Orangery,
  Graveyard-18
Wye Oak, Talbot County-20

PENNSYLV
Ye HILL BILLY
THAR'S COAL IN THEM HILLS
MAPLE SYRUP and BUCKWHEAT, TOO CAKES
TALL TIMBER
DEEP CREEK Lake
CUMBERLAND
A PLEASANT PLACE
HAGERSTOWN
A PLEASANT PLACE, TOO.
APPLE ORCHARDS
(PEACHES, TOO)
"WHO TOUCHES ONE HAI OF YON GRAY HEAD..."
FREDERICK
A JOLLY EARLY GERMAN SETTLER
FRONTIER DAYS
THE HUNTIN
Many Fertile Farms
Ye Hotte Air
WASHINGTON SUBURBS
WASHINGTON
THEE SH NOT ST MY LIBER
A FEDERAL JOBHOLDER
Lily Dasche
AN EARLY SETTLER FRATERNIZES
YE SHOCKED DESCENDANT OF TODAY
YUM! CHICKEN MARYLAND
GIANT DRUMSTICK
29th DIVISION
Ye ORIOLE
NOT DRAWN TO SCALE
Ye MAP of MARYLAND
PROUD FREE State on the GREAT Chesapeake
Ye SEAFOOD, SOLE★ FARE of MANY NATIVES
★HA! Ye PUN!
OL' VIRGINNY